Yet stay, let me not rashly call in doubt
Divine Prediction; what if all foretold
Had been fulfilld but through mine own default,
Whom have I to complain of but my self?
Who this high gift of strength committed to me,
In what part lodg'd, how easily bereft me,
Under the Seal of silence could not keep,
But weakly to a woman must reveal it
O'recome with importunity and tears.
O impotence of mind, in body strong!
But what is strength without a double share
Of wisdom, vast, unwieldy, burdensom,
Proudly secure, yet liable to fall
By weakest suttleties, not made to rule,
But to subserve where wisdom bears command.
God, when he gave me strength, to shew withal
How slight the gift was, hung it in my Hair.
But peace, I must not quarrel with the will
Of highest dispensation, which herein
Happ'ly had ends above my reach to know:
Suffices that to me strength is my bane,
And proves the sourse of all my miseries;
So many, and so huge, that each apart
Would ask a life to wail, but chief of all,
O loss of sight, of thee I most complain!
Blind among enemies, O worse then chains,
Dungeon, or beggery, or decrepit age!
Light the prime work of God to me is extinct,
And all her various objects of delight
Annull'd, which might in part my grief have eas'd,
Inferiour to the vilest now become
Of man or worm; the vilest here excel me,
They creep, yet see, I dark in light expos'd
To daily fraud, contempt, abuse and wrong,
Within doors, or without, still as a fool,
In power of others, never in my own;
Scarce half I seem to live, dead more then half.
O dark, dark, dark, amid the blaze of noon,
Irrecoverably dark, total Eclipse
Without all hope of day!
O first created Beam, and thou great Word,
Let there be light, and light was over all;
Why am I thus bereav'd thy prime decree?
The Sun to me is dark
And silent as the Moon,
When she deserts the night
Hid in her vacant interlunar cave.
Since light so necessary is to life,
And almost life itself, if it be true
That light is in the Soul,
She all in every part; why was the sight

To such a tender ball as th' eye confin'd?
So obvious and so easie to be quench't,
And not as feeling through all parts diffus'd,
That she might look at will through every pore?
Then had I not been thus exil'd from light;
As in the land of darkness yet in light,
To live a life half dead, a living death,
And buried; but O yet more miserable!
My self, my Sepulcher, a moving Grave,
Buried, yet not exempt
By priviledge of death and burial
From worst of other evils, pains and wrongs,
But made hereby obnoxious more
To all the miseries of life,
Life in captivity
Among inhuman foes.
But who are these? for with joint pace I hear
The tread of many feet stearing this way;
Perhaps my enemies who come to stare
At my affliction, and perhaps to insult,
Thir daily practice to afflict me more.

CHORUS
This, this is he; softly a while,
Let us not break in upon him;
O change beyond report, thought, or belief!
See how he lies at random, carelessly diffus'd,
With languish't head unpropt,
As one past hope, abandon'd
And by himself given over;
In slavish habit, ill-fitted weeds
O're worn and soild;
Or do my eyes misrepresent? Can this be hee,
That Heroic, that Renown'd,
Irresistible Samson? whom unarm'd
No strength of man, or fiercest wild beast could withstand;
Who tore the Lion, as the Lion tears the Kid,
Ran on embattelld Armies clad in Iron,
And weaponless himself,
Made Arms ridiculous, useless the forgery
Of brazen shield and spear, the hammer'd Cuirass,
Chalybean temper'd steel, and frock of mail
Adamantean Proof;
But safest he who stood aloof,
When insupportably his foot advanc't,
In scorn of thir proud arms and warlike tools,
Spurn'd them to death by Troops. The bold Ascalonite
Fled from his Lion ramp, old Warriors turn'd
Their plated backs under his heel;
Or grovling soild thir crested helmets in the dust.
Then with what trivial weapon came to Hand,

Samson Agonistes & Lycidas by John Milton

John Milton was born in Bread Street, London, on December 9th, 1608. His early years were privately tutored before gaining a place at St Paul's School and in 1625 he matriculated at Christ's College, Cambridge, earning a BA in 1629 and an MA in 1632. At Cambridge he had developed a reputation for poetic skill but also experienced alienation from his peers and university life as a whole.

The next 6 years were spent in private study. He read both ancient and modern works of theology, philosophy, history, politics, literature and science, in preparation for a poetical career. Milton mastered Latin, Greek, Hebrew, French, Spanish, and Italian. To these he would add Old English (whilst researching his History of Britain) and also acquired more than a passing acquaintance in Dutch.

Although he was studying, some of his poetry from this time is remarkable; L'Allegro and Il Penseroso in 1631 and Lycidias in 1638.

In May 1638, Milton embarked upon a 15-month tour of France and Italy. These travels added a new and direct experience of artistic and religious traditions, especially Roman Catholicism. He cut the journey short to return home during the summer of 1639 because of what he claimed were "sad tidings of civil war in England."

Once home, Milton wrote prose tracts against episcopacy, in the service of the Puritan and Parliamentary cause.

He married 16-year-old Mary Powell in June 1643 but she left him after only a few months during which he wrote and published several writings on divorce. Mary did return after 3 years and their life thereafter seemed harmonious. Milton received a hostile response to the divorce tracts and drove him to write Areopagitica, his celebrated attack on pre-printing censorship.

With the parliamentary victory in the Civil War, Milton wrote The Tenure of Kings and Magistrates (1649) which defended popular government and implicitly sanctioned the regicide which led to his appointment as Secretary for Foreign Tongues by the Council of State.

On 24 February 1652 Milton published his Latin defense of the English People, Defensio Pro Populo Anglicano, also known as the First Defense. Milton's Latin prose and intellectual sweep, quickly gained him a European reputation.

Tragically his first wife, Mary, died on May 5th, 1652 following the birth of their fourth child. The following year Milton had become totally blind, probably due to glaucoma. He then had to dictate his verse and prose to helpers, one of whom was the poet Andrew Marvell.

He married again to Katherine Woodcock but she died in February 1658, less than four months after giving birth to a daughter, who also tragically died.

Though Cromwell's death in 1658 caused the English Republic to collapse Milton stubbornly clung to his beliefs and in 1659 he published A Treatise of Civil Power, attacking the concept of a state-dominated church. Upon the Restoration in May 1660, Milton went into hiding for his life. An arrest warrant was issued and his writings burnt. He re-emerged after a general pardon was issued, but was nevertheless arrested and briefly imprisoned before influential friends, such as Marvell, now an MP, intervened

His third marriage was to Elizabeth Mynshull. Despite a 31-year age gap, the marriage seemed happy and Milton spent the remaining decade of his life living quietly in London, apart from a short spell in Chalfont St. Giles, during the Great Plague of London.

Milton was to now publish his greatest works, which had been gestating for many years. Paradise Lost, perhaps the classic English Epic poem was originally published in 10 books in 1667. This was followed by Paradise Regained and Samson Agonistes in 1671. Because of his anti-monarchy views their reception was muted but over the centuries since Milton has established himself as second only to Shakespeare. He died of kidney failure on November 8th, 1674 and was buried in the church of St Giles Cripplegate.

Index of Contents

SAMSON AGONISTES, A DRAMATIC POEM

Of that sort of Dramatic Poem which is call'd Tragedy.

Tragedy, as it was antiently compos'd, hath been ever held the gravest, moralest, and most profitable of all other Poems: therefore said by Aristotle to be of power by raising pity and fear, or terror, to purge the mind of those and such like passions, that is to temper and reduce them to just measure with a kind of delight, stirr'd up by reading or seeing those passions well imitated. Nor is Nature wanting in her own effects to make good his assertion: for so in Physic things of melancholic hue and quality are us'd against melancholy, sowr against sowr, salt to remove salt humours.

Hence Philosophers and other gravest Writers, as Cicero, Plutarch and others, frequently cite out of Tragic Poets, both to adorn and illustrate thir discourse. The Apostle Paul himself thought it not unworthy to insert a verse of Euripides into the Text of Holy Scripture, I Cor. . . and Paraeus commenting on the Revelation, divides the whole Book as a Tragedy, into Acts distinguisht each by a Chorus of Heavenly Harpings and Song between. Heretofore Men in highest dignity have labour'd not a little to be thought able to compose a Tragedy. Of that honour Dionysius the elder was no less ambitious, then before of his attaining to the Tyranny. Augustus Caesar also had begun his Ajax, but unable to please his own judgment with what he had begun. left it unfinisht. Seneca the Philosopher is by some thought the Author of those Tragedies (at lest the best of them) that go under that name. Gregory Nazianzen a Father of the Church, thought it not unbeseeming the sanctity of his person to write a Tragedy which he entitl'd, Christ suffering. This is mention'd to vindicate Tragedy from the small esteem, or rather infamy, which in the account of many it undergoes at this day with other common Interludes; hap'ning through the Poets error of intermixing Comic stuff with Tragic sadness and gravity; or introducing trivial and vulgar persons, which by all judicious hath bin counted absurd; and brought in without discretion, corruptly to gratifie the people. And though antient Tragedy use no Prologue, yet using sometimes, in case of self defence, or explanation, that which Martial calls an Epistle; in behalf of this Tragedy coming forth after the antient manner, much different from what among us passes for best, thus much before-hand may be Epistl'd; that Chorus is here introduc'd after the Greek manner, not antient only but modern, and still in use among the Italians. In the modelling therefore of this Poem with good reason, the Antients and Italians are rather follow'd, as of much more authority and fame. The measure of Verse us'd in the Chorus is of all sorts, call'd by the Greeks Monostrophic, or rather Apolelymenon, without regard had to Strophe, Antistrophe or Epod, which were a kind of Stanza's fram'd only for the Music, then us'd with the Chorus that sung; not essential to the Poem, and therefore not material; or being divided into Stanza's or Pauses they may be call'd Allaeostropha. Division into Act and Scene referring chiefly to the Stage (to which this work never was intended) is here omitted.

It suffices if the whole Drama be found not produc't beyond the fift Act, of the style and uniformitie, and that commonly call'd the Plot, whether intricate or explicit, which is nothing indeed but such economy, or disposition of the fable as may stand best with verisimilitude and decorum; they only will best judge who are not unacquainted with Aeschulus, Sophocles, and Euripides, the three Tragic Poets unequall'd yet by any, and the best rule to all who endeavour to write Tragedy. The circumscription of time wherein the whole Drama begins and ends, is according to antient rule, and best example, within the space of hours.

The ARGUMENT

Samson made Captive, Blind, and now in the Prison at Gaza, there to labour as in a common work-house, on a Festival day, in the general cessation from labour, comes forth into the open Air, to a place nigh, somewhat retir'd there to sit a while and bemoan his condition. Where he happens at length to be visited by certain friends and equals of his tribe, which make the Chorus, who seek to comfort him what they can; then by his old Father Manoa, who endeavours the like, and withal tells him his purpose to procure his liberty by ransom; lastly, that this Feast was proclaim'd by the Philistins as a day of Thanksgiving for thir deliverance from the hands of Samson, which yet more troubles him. Manoa then departs to prosecute his endeavour with the Philistian Lords for Samson's redemption; who in the mean while is visited by other persons; and lastly by a publick Officer to require coming to the Feast before the Lords and People, to play or shew his strength in thir presence; he at first refuses, dismissing the publick officer with absolute denyal to come; at length perswaded inwardly that this was from God, he yields to go along with him, who came now the second time with great threatnings to fetch him; the Chorus yet remaining on the place, Manoa returns full of joyful hope, to procure e're long his Sons deliverance: in the midst of which discourse an Ebrew comes in haste confusedly at first; and afterward more distinctly relating the Catastrophe, what Samson had done to the Philistins, and by accident to himself; wherewith the Tragedy ends.

THE PERSONS

Samson
Manoa the father of Samson
Dalila his wife
Harapha of Gath

Publick Officer
Messenger
Chorus of Danites

THE SCENE – BEFORE THE PRISON IN GAZA

SAMSON
A little onward lend thy guiding hand
To these dark steps, a little further on;
For yonder bank hath choice of Sun or shade,
There I am wont to sit, when any chance
Relieves me from my task of servile toyl,
Daily in the common Prison else enjoyn'd me,
Where I a Prisoner chain'd, scarce freely draw
The air imprison'd also, close and damp,
Unwholsom draught: but here I feel amends,
The breath of Heav'n fresh-blowing, pure and sweet,
With day-spring born; here leave me to respire.
This day a solemn Feast the people hold
To Dagon thir Sea-Idol, and forbid
Laborious works, unwillingly this rest
Thir Superstition yields me; hence with leave
Retiring from the popular noise, I seek
This unfrequented place to find some ease,
Ease to the body some, none to the mind
From restless thoughts, that like a deadly swarm
Of Hornets arm'd, no sooner found alone,
But rush upon me thronging, and present
Times past, what once I was, and what am now.
O wherefore was my birth from Heaven foretold
Twice by an Angel, who at last in sight
Of both my Parents all in flames ascended
From off the Altar, where an Off'ring burn'd,
As in a fiery column charioting
His Godlike presence, and from some great act
Or benefit reveal'd to Abraham's race?
Why was my breeding order'd and prescrib'd
As of a person separate to God,
Design'd for great exploits; if I must dye
Betray'd, Captiv'd, and both my Eyes put out,
Made of my Enemies the scorn and gaze;
To grind in Brazen Fetters under task
With this Heav'n-gifted strength? O glorious strength
Put to the labour of a Beast, debas't
Lower then bondslave! Promise was that I
Should Israel from Philistian yoke deliver;
Ask for this great Deliverer now, and find him
Eyeless in Gaza at the Mill with slaves,
Himself in bonds under Philistian yoke;

The Jaw of a dead Ass, his sword of bone,
A thousand fore-skins fell, the flower of Palestin
In Ramath-lechi famous to this day:
Then by main force pull'd up, and on his shoulders bore
The Gates of Azza, Post, and massie Bar
Up to the Hill by Hebron, seat of Giants old,
No journey of a Sabbath day, and loaded so;
Like whom the Gentiles feign to bear up Heav'n.
Which shall I first bewail,
Thy Bondage or lost Sight,
Prison within Prison
Inseparably dark?
Thou art become (O worst imprisonment!)
The Dungeon of thy self; thy Soul
 (Which Men enjoying sight oft without cause complain)
Imprison'd now indeed,
In real darkness of the body dwells,
Shut up from outward light
To incorporate with gloomy night;
For inward light alas
Puts forth no visual beam.
O mirror of our fickle state,
Since man on earth unparallel'd!
The rarer thy example stands,
By how much from the top of wondrous glory,
Strongest of mortal men,
To lowest pitch of abject fortune thou art fall'n.
For him I reckon not in high estate
Whom long descent of birth
Or the sphear of fortune raises;
But thee whose strength, while vertue was her mate
Might have subdu'd the Earth,
Universally crown'd with highest praises.

SAMSON
I hear the sound of words, thir sense the air
Dissolves unjointed e're it reach my ear.

CHORUS
Hee speaks, let us draw nigh. Matchless in might,
The glory late of Israel, now the grief;
We come thy friends and neighbours not unknown
From Eshtaol and Zora's fruitful Vale
To visit or bewail thee, or if better,
Counsel or Consolation we may bring,
Salve to thy Sores, apt words have power to swage
The tumors of a troubl'd mind,
And are as Balm to fester'd wounds.

SAMSON
Your coming, Friends, revives me, for I learn

Now of my own experience, not by talk,
How counterfeit a coin they are who friends
Bear in their Superscription (of the most
I would be understood) in prosperous days
They swarm, but in adverse withdraw their head
Not to be found, though sought. Wee see, O friends.
How many evils have enclos'd me round;
Yet that which was the worst now least afflicts me,
Blindness, for had I sight, confus'd with shame,
How could I once look up, or heave the head,
Who like a foolish Pilot have shipwrack't,
My Vessel trusted to me from above,
Gloriously rigg'd; and for a word, a tear,
Fool, have divulg'd the secret gift of God
To a deceitful Woman: tell me Friends,
Am I not sung and proverbd for a Fool
In every street, do they not say, how well
Are come upon him his deserts? yet why?
Immeasurable strength they might behold
In me, of wisdom nothing more then mean;
This with the other should, at least, have paird,
These two proportiond ill drove me transverse.

CHORUS
Tax not divine disposal, wisest Men
Have err'd, and by bad Women been deceiv'd;
And shall again, pretend they ne're so wise.
Deject not then so overmuch thy self,
Who hast of sorrow thy full load besides;
Yet truth to say, I oft have heard men wonder
Why thou shouldst wed Philistian women rather
Then of thine own Tribe fairer, or as fair,
At least of thy own Nation, and as noble.

SAMSON
The first I saw at Timna, and she pleas'd
Mee, not my Parents, that I sought to wed,
The daughter of an Infidel: they knew not
That what I motion'd was of God; I knew
From intimate impulse, and therefore urg'd
The Marriage on; that by occasion hence
I might begin Israel's Deliverance,
The work to which I was divinely call'd;
She proving false, the next I took to Wife
(O that I never had! fond wish too late)
Was in the Vale of Sorec, Dalila,
That specious Monster, my accomplisht snare.
I thought it lawful from my former act,
And the same end; still watching to oppress
Israel's oppressours: of what now I suffer
She was not the prime cause, but I my self,

Who vanquisht with a peal of words (O weakness!)
Gave up my fort of silence to a Woman.

CHORUS
In seeking just occasion to provoke
The Philistine, thy Countries Enemy,
Thou never wast remiss, I hear thee witness:
Yet Israel still serves with all his Sons.

SAMSON
That fault I take not on me, but transfer
On Israel's Governours, and Heads of Tribes,
Who seeing those great acts which God had done
Singly by me against their Conquerours
Acknowledg'd not, or not at all consider'd
Deliverance offerd: I on th' other side
Us'd no ambition to commend my deeds,
The deeds themselves, though mute, spoke loud the dooer;
But they persisted deaf, and would not seem
To count them things worth notice, till at length
Thir Lords the Philistines with gather'd powers
Enterd Judea seeking mee, who then
Safe to the rock of Etham was retir'd,
Not flying, but fore-casting in what place
To set upon them, what advantag'd best;
Mean while the men of Judah to prevent
The harrass of thir Land, beset me round;
I willingly on some conditions came
Into thir hands, and they as gladly yield me
To the uncircumcis'd a welcom prey,
Bound with two cords; but cords to me were threds
Toucht with the flame: on thir whole Host I flew
Unarm'd, and with a trivial weapon fell'd
Thir choicest youth; they only liv'd who fled.
Had Judah that day join'd, or one whole Tribe,
They had by this possess'd the Towers of Gath,
And lorded over them whom now they serve;
But what more oft in Nations grown corrupt,
And by thir vices brought to servitude,
Then to love Bondage more then Liberty,
Bondage with ease then strenuous liberty;
And to despise, or envy, or suspect
Whom God hath of his special favour rais'd
As thir Deliverer; if he aught begin,
How frequent to desert him, and at last
To heap ingratitude on worthiest deeds?

CHORUS
Thy words to my remembrance bring
How Succoth and the Fort of Penuel
Thir great Deliverer contemn'd,

The matchless Gideon in pursuit
Of Madian and her vanquisht Kings;
And how ingrateful Ephraim
Not worse then by his shield and spear
Had dealt with Jephtha, who by argument,
Defended Israel from the Ammonite,
Had not his prowess quell'd thir pride
In that sore battel when so many dy'd
Without Reprieve adjudg'd to death,
For want of well pronouncing Shibboleth.

SAMSON
Of such examples adde mee to the roul,
Mee easily indeed mine may neglect,
But Gods propos'd deliverance not so.

CHORUS
Just are the ways of God,
And justifiable to Men;
Unless there be who think not God at all,
If any be, they walk obscure;
For of such Doctrine never was there School,
But the heart of the Fool,
And no man therein Doctor but himself.
Yet more there be who doubt his ways not just,
As to his own edicts, found contradicting,
Then give the rains to wandring thought,
Regardless of his glories diminution;
Till by thir own perplexities involv'd
They ravel more, still less resolv'd,
But never find self-satisfying solution.
As if they would confine th' interminable,
And tie him to his own prescript,
Who made our Laws to bind us, not himself,
And hath full right to exempt
Whom so it pleases him by choice
From National obstriction, without taint
Of sin, or legal debt;
For with his own Laws he can best dispence.
He would not else who never wanted means,
Nor in respect of the enemy just cause
To set his people free,
Have prompted this Heroic Nazarite,
Against his vow of strictest purity,
To seek in marriage that fallacious Bride,
Unclean, unchaste.
Down Reason then, at least vain reasonings down,
Though Reason here aver
That moral verdit quits her of unclean:
Unchaste was subsequent, her stain not his.
But see here comes thy reverend Sire

With careful step, Locks white as doune,
Old Manoah: advise
Forthwith how thou oughtst to receive him.

SAMSON

Ay me, another inward grief awak't,
With mention of that name renews th' assault.

MANOA

Brethren and men of Dan, for such ye seem,
Though in this uncouth place; if old respect,
As I suppose, towards your once gloried friend,
My Son now Captive, hither hath inform'd
Your younger feet, while mine cast back with age
Came lagging after; say if he be here.

CHORUS

As signal now in low dejected state,
As earst in highest; behold him where be lies.

MANOA

O miserable change! is this the man,
That invincible Samson, far renown'd,
The dread of Israel's foes, who with a strength
Equivalent to Angels walk'd thir streets,
None offering fight; who single combatant
Duell'd thir Armies rank't in proud array,
Himself an Army, now unequal match
To save himself against a coward arm'd
At one spears length. O ever failing trust
In mortal strength! and oh what not in man
Deceivable and vain! Nay what thing good
Pray'd for, but often proves our woe, our bane?
I pray'd for Children, and thought barrenness
In wedlock a reproach; I gain'd a Son,
And such a Son as all Men hail'd me happy;
Who would be now a Father in my stead?
O wherefore did God grant me my request,
And as a blessing with such pomp adorn'd?
Why are his gifts desirable, to tempt
Our earnest Prayers, then giv'n with solemn hand
As Graces, draw a Scorpions tail behind?
For this did the Angel twice descend? for this
Ordain'd thy nurture holy, as of a Plant;
Select, and Sacred, Glorious for a while,
The miracle of men: then in an hour
Ensnar'd, assaulted, overcome, led bound,
Thy Foes derision, Captive, Poor, and Blind
Into a Dungeon thrust, to work with Slaves?
Alas methinks whom God hath chosen once
To worthiest deeds, if he through frailty err,

He should not so o'rewhelm, and as a thrall
Subject him to so foul indignities,
Be it but for honours sake of former deeds.

SAMSON
Appoint not heavenly disposition, Father,
Nothing of all these evils hath befall'n me
But justly; I my self have brought them on,
Sole Author I, sole cause: if aught seem vile,
As vile hath been my folly, who have profan'd
The mystery of God giv'n me under pledge
Of vow, and have betray'd it to a woman,
A Canaanite, my faithless enemy.
This well I knew, nor was at all surpris'd,
But warn'd by oft experience: did not she
Of Timna first betray me, and reveal
The secret wrested from me in her highth
Of Nuptial Love profest, carrying it strait
To them who had corrupted her, my Spies,
And Rivals? In this other was there found
More Faith? who also in her prime of love,
Spousal embraces, vitiated with Gold,
Though offer'd only, by the sent conceiv'd
Her spurious first-born; Treason against me?
Thrice she assay'd with flattering prayers and sighs,
And amorous reproaches to win from me
My capital secret, in what part my strength
Lay stor'd in what part summ'd, that she might know:
Thrice I deluded her, and turn'd to sport
Her importunity, each time perceiving
How openly, and with what impudence
She purpos'd to betray me, and (which was worse
Then undissembl'd hate) with what contempt
She sought to make me Traytor to my self;
Yet the fourth time, when mustring all her wiles,
With blandisht parlies, feminine assaults,
Tongue-batteries, she surceas'd not day nor night
To storm me over-watch't, and wearied out.
At times when men seek most repose and rest,
I yielded, and unlock'd her all my heart,
Who with a grain of manhood well resolv'd
Might easily have shook off all her snares:
But foul effeminacy held me yok't
Her Bond-slave; O indignity, O blot
To Honour and Religion! servil mind
Rewarded well with servil punishment!
The base degree to which I now am fall'n,
These rags, this grinding, is not yet so base
As was my former servitude, ignoble,
Unmanly, ignominious, infamous,
True slavery, and that blindness worse then this,

That saw not how degeneratly I serv'd.

MANOA

I cannot praise thy Marriage choises, Son,
Rather approv'd them not; but thou didst plead
Divine impulsion prompting how thou might'st
Find some occasion to infest our Foes.
I state not that; this I am sure; our Foes
Found soon occasion thereby to make thee
Thir Captive, and thir triumph; thou the sooner
Temptation found'st, or over-potent charms
To violate the sacred trust of silence
Deposited within thee; which to have kept
Tacit, was in thy power; true; and thou hear'st
Enough, and more the burden of that fault;
Bitterly hast thou paid, and still art paying
That rigid score. A worse thing yet remains,
This day the Philistines a popular Feast
Here celebrate in Gaza, and proclaim
Great Pomp, and Sacrifice, and Praises loud
To Dagon, as their God who hath deliver'd
Thee Samson bound and blind into thir hands,
Them out of thine, who slew'st them many a slain.
So Dagon shall be magnifi'd, and God,
Besides whom is no God, compar'd with Idols,
Disglorifi'd, blasphem'd, and had in scorn
By th' Idolatrous rout amidst thir wine;
Which to have come to pass by means of thee,
Samson, of all thy sufferings think the heaviest,
Of all reproach the most with shame that ever
Could have befall'n thee and thy Fathers house.

SAMSON

Father, I do acknowledge and confess
That I this honour, I this pomp have brought
To Dagon, and advanc'd his praises high
Among the Heathen round; to God have brought
Dishonour, obloquie, and op't the mouths
Of Idolists, and Atheists; have brought scandal
To Israel diffidence of God, and doubt
In feeble hearts, propense anough before
To waver, or fall off and joyn with Idols:
Which is my chief affliction, shame and sorrow,
The anguish of my Soul, that suffers not
Mine eie to harbour sleep, or thoughts to rest.
This only hope relieves me, that the strife
With me hath end; all the contest is now
'Twixt God and Dagon; Dagon hath presum'd,
Me overthrown, to enter lists with God,
His Deity comparing and preferring
Before the God of Abraham. He, he sure,

Will not connive, or linger, thus provok'd,
But will arise and his great name assert:
Dagon must stoop, and shall e're long receive
Such a discomfit, as shall quite despoil him
Of all these boasted Trophies won on me,
And with confusion blank his Worshippers.

MANOA
With cause this hope relieves thee, and these words
I as a Prophecy receive: for God,
Nothing more certain, will not long defer
To vindicate the glory of his name
Against all competition, nor will long
Endure it, doubtful whether God be Lord,
Or Dagon. But for thee what shall be done?
Thou must not in the mean while here forgot
Lie in this miserable loathsom plight
Neglected. I already have made way
To some Philistian Lords, with whom to treat
About thy ransom: well they may by this
Have satisfi'd thir utmost of revenge
By pains and slaveries, worse then death inflicted
On thee, who now no more canst do them harm.

SAMSON
Spare that proposal, Father, spare the trouble
Of that sollicitation; let me here,
As I deserve, pay on my punishment;
And expiate, if possible, my crime,
Shameful garrulity. To have reveal'd
Secrets of men, the secrets of a friend,
How hainous had the fact been, how deserving
Contempt, and scorn of all, to be excluded
All friendship, and avoided as a blab,
The mark of fool set on his front?
But I Gods counsel have not kept, his holy secret
Presumptuously have publish'd, impiously,
Weakly at least, and shamefully: A sin
That Gentiles in thir Parables condemn
To thir abyss and horrid pains confin'd.

MANOA
Be penitent and for thy fault contrite,
But act not in thy own affliction, Son,
Repent the sin, but if the punishment
Thou canst avoid, selfpreservation bids;
Or th' execution leave to high disposal,
And let another hand, not thine, exact
Thy penal forfeit from thy self; perhaps
God will relent, and quit thee all his debt;
Who evermore approves and more accepts

(Best pleas'd with humble and filial submission)
Him who imploring mercy sues for life,
Then who selfrigorous chooses death as due;
Which argues overjust, and self-displeas'd
For self-offence, more then for God offended.
Reject not then what offerd means, who knows
But God hath set before us, to return thee
Home to thy countrey and his sacred house,
Where thou mayst bring thy off'rings, to avert
His further ire, with praiers and vows renew'd.

SAMSON

His pardon I implore; but as for life,
To what end should I seek it? when in strength
All mortals I excell'd, and great in hopes
With youthful courage and magnanimous thoughts
Of birth from Heav'n foretold and high exploits,
Full of divine instinct, after some proof
Of acts indeed heroic, far beyond
The Sons of Anac, famous now and blaz'd,
Fearless of danger, like a petty God
I walk'd about admir'd of all and dreaded
On hostile ground, none daring my affront.
Then swoll'n with pride into the snare I fell
Of fair fallacious looks, venereal trains,
Softn'd with pleasure and voluptuous life;
At length to lay my head and hallow'd pledge
Of all my strength in the lascivious lap
Of a deceitful Concubine who shore me
Like a tame Weather, all my precious fleece,
Then turn'd me out ridiculous, despoil'd,
Shav'n, and disarm'd among my enemies.

CHORUS

Desire of wine and all delicious drinks,
Which many a famous Warriour overturns,
Thou couldst repress, nor did the dancing Rubie
Sparkling; out-pow'rd, the flavor, or the smell,
Or taste that cheers the heart of Gods and men,
Allure thee from the cool Crystalline stream.

SAMSON

Where ever fountain or fresh current flow'd
Against the Eastern ray, translucent, pure,
With touch aetherial of Heav'ns fiery rod
I drank, from the clear milkie juice allaying
Thirst, and refresht; nor envy'd them the grape
Whose heads that turbulent liquor fills with fumes.

CHORUS

O madness, to think use of strongest wines

And strongest drinks our chief support of health,
When God with these forbid'n made choice to rear
His mighty Champion, strong above compare,
Whose drink was only from the liquid brook.

SAMSON
But what avail'd this temperance, not compleat
Against another object more enticing?
What boots it at one gate to make defence,
And at another to let in the foe
Effeminatly vanquish't? by which means,
Now blind, disheartn'd, sham'd, dishonour'd, quell'd,
To what can I be useful, wherein serve
My Nation, and the work from Heav'n impos'd,
But to sit idle on the houshold hearth,
A burdenous drone; to visitants a gaze,
Or pitied object, these redundant locks
Robustious to no purpose clustring down,
Vain monument of strength; till length of years
And sedentary numness craze my limbs
To a contemptible old age obscure.
Here rather let me drudge and earn my bread,
Till vermin or the draff of servil food
Consume me, and oft-invocated death
Hast'n the welcom end of all my pains.

MANOA
Wilt thou then serve the Philistines with that gift
Which was expresly giv'n thee to annoy them?
Better at home lie bed-rid, not only idle,
Inglorious, unimploy'd, with age out-worn.
But God who caus'd a fountain at thy prayer
From the dry ground to spring, thy thirst to allay
After the brunt of battel, can as easie
Cause light again within thy eies to spring,
Wherewith to serve him better then thou hast;
And I perswade me so; why else this strength
Miraculous yet remaining in those locks?
His might continues in thee not for naught,
Nor shall his wondrous gifts be frustrate thus.

SAMSON
All otherwise to me my thoughts portend,
That these dark orbs no more shall treat with light,
Nor th' other light of life continue long,
But yield to double darkness nigh at hand:
So much I feel my genial spirits droop,
My hopes all flat, nature within me seems
In all her functions weary of herself;
My race of glory run, and race of shame,
And I shall shortly be with them that rest.

MANOA

Believe not these suggestions which proceed
From anguish of the mind and humours black,
That mingle with thy fancy. I however
Must not omit a Fathers timely care
To prosecute the means of thy deliverance
By ransom or how else: mean while be calm,
And healing words from these thy friends admit.

SAMSON

O that torment should not be confin'd
To the bodies wounds and sores
With maladies innumerable
In heart, head, brest, and reins;
But must secret passage find
To th' inmost mind,
There exercise all his fierce accidents,
And on her purest spirits prey,
As on entrails, joints, and limbs,
With answerable pains, but more intense,
'Though void of corporal sense.
My griefs not only pain me
As a lingring disease,
But finding no redress, ferment and rage,
Nor less then wounds immedicable
Ranckle, and fester, and gangrene,
To black mortification.
Thoughts my Tormenters arm'd with deadly stings
Mangle my apprehensive tenderest parts,
Exasperate, exulcerate, and raise
Dire inflammation which no cooling herb
Or rnedcinal liquor can asswage,
Nor breath of Vernal Air from snowy Alp.
Sleep hath forsook and giv'n me o're
To deaths benumming Opium as my only cure.
Thence faintings, swounings of despair,
And sense of Heav'ns desertion.
I was his nursling once and choice delight,
His destin'd from the womb,
Promisd by Heavenly message twice descending.
Under his special eie
Abstemious I grew up and thriv'd amain;
He led me on to mightiest deeds
Above the nerve of mortal arm
Against the uncircumcis'd, our enemies.
But now hath cast me off as never known,
And to those cruel enemies,
Whom I by his appointment had provok't,
Left me all helpless with th' irreparable loss
Of sight, reserv'd alive to be repeated

The subject of thir cruelty, or scorn.
Nor am I in the list of them that hope;
Hopeless are all my evils, all remediless;
This one prayer yet remains, might I be heard,
No long petition, speedy death,
The close of all my miseries, and the balm.

CHORUS
Many are the sayings of the wise
In antient and in modern books enroll'd;
Extolling Patience as the truest fortitude;
And to the bearing well of all calamities,
All chances incident to mans frail life
Consolatories writ
With studied argument, and much perswasion sought
Lenient of grief and anxious thought,
But with th' afflicted in his pangs thir sound
Little prevails, or rather seems a tune,
Harsh, and of dissonant mood from his complaint,
Unless he feel within
Some sourse of consolation from above;
Secret refreshings, that repair his strength,
And fainting spirits uphold.
God of our Fathers, what is man!
That thou towards him with hand so various,
Or might I say contrarious,
Temperst thy providence through his short course,
Not evenly, as thou rul'st
The Angelic orders and inferiour creatures mute,
Irrational and brute.
Nor do I name of men the common rout,
That wandring loose about
Grow up and perish, as the summer flie,
Heads without name no more rememberd,
But such as thou hast solemnly elected,
With gifts and graces eminently adorn'd
To some great work, thy glory,
And peoples safety, which in part they effect:
Yet toward these thus dignifi'd, thou oft
Amidst thir highth of noon,
Changest thy countenance, and thy hand with no regard
Of highest favours past
From thee on them, or them to thee of service.
Nor only dost degrade them, or remit
To life obscur'd, which were a fair dismission,
But throw'st them lower then thou didst exalt them high,
Unseemly falls in human eie,
Too grievous for the trespass or omission,
Oft leav'st them to the hostile sword
Of Heathen and prophane, thir carkasses
To dogs and fowls a prey, or else captiv'd:

Or to the unjust tribunals, under change of times,
And condemnation of the ingrateful multitude.
If these they scape, perhaps in poverty
With sickness and disease thou bow'st them down,
Painful diseases and deform'd,
In crude old age;
Though not disordinate, yet causless suffring
The punishment of dissolute days, in fine,
Just or unjust, alike seem miserable,
For oft alike, both come to evil end.
So deal not with this once thy glorious Champion,
The Image of thy strength, and mighty minister.
What do I beg? how hast thou dealt already?
Behold him in this state calamitous, and turn
His labours, for thou canst, to peaceful end.
But who is this, what thing of Sea or Land?
Femal of sex it seems,
That so bedeckt, ornate, and gay,
Comes this way sailing
Like a stately Ship
Of Tarsus, bound for th' Isles
Of Javan or Gadier
With all her bravery on, and tackle trim,
Sails fill'd, and streamers waving,
Courted by all the winds that hold them play,
An Amber sent of odorous perfume
Her harbinger, a damsel train behind;
Some rich Philistian Matron she may seem,
And now at nearer view, no other certain
Than Dalila thy wife.

SAMSON
My Wife, my Traytress, let her not come near me.

CHORUS
Yet on she moves, now stands & eies thee fixt,
About t'have spoke, but now, with head declin'd
Like a fair flower surcharg'd with dew, she weeps
And words addrest seem into tears dissolv'd,
Wetting the borders of her silk'n veil:
But now again she makes address to speak.

DALILA
With doubtful feet and wavering resolution
I came, still dreading thy displeasure, Samson,
Which to have merited, without excuse,
I cannot but acknowledge; yet if tears
May expiate (though the fact more evil drew
In the perverse event then I foresaw)
My penance hath not slack'n'd, though my pardon
No way assur'd. But conjugal affection

Prevailing over fear, and timerous doubt
Hath led me on desirous to behold
Once more thy face, and know of thy estate.
If aught in my ability may serve
To light'n what thou suffer'st, and appease
Thy mind with what amends is in my power,
Though late, yet in some part to recompense
My rash but more unfortunate misdeed.

SAMSON

Out, out Hyaena; these are thy wonted arts,
And arts of every woman false like thee,
To break all faith, all vows, deceive, betray,
Then as repentant to submit, beseech,
And reconcilement move with feign'd remorse,
Confess, and promise wonders in her change,
Not truly penitent, but chief to try
Her husband, how far urg'd his patience bears,
His vertue or weakness which way to assail:
Then with more cautious and instructed skill
Again transgresses, and again submits;
That wisest and best men full oft beguil'd
With goodness principl'd not to reject
The penitent, but ever to forgive,
Are drawn to wear out miserable days,
Entangl'd with a poysnous bosom snake,
If not by quick destruction soon cut off
As I by thee, to Ages an example.

DALILA

Yet hear me Samson; not that I endeavour
To lessen or extenuate my offence,
But that on th' other side if it be weigh'd
By it self, with aggravations not surcharg'd,
Or else with just allowance counterpois'd
I may, if possible, thy pardon find
The easier towards me, or thy hatred less.
First granting, as I do, it was a weakness
In me, but incident to all our sex,
Curiosity, inquisitive, importune
Of secrets, then with like infirmity
To publish them, both common female faults:
Was it not weakness also to make known
For importunity, that is for naught,
Wherein consisted all thy strength and safety?
To what I did thou shewdst me first the way.
But I to enemies reveal'd, and should not.
Nor shouldst thou have trusted that to womans frailty
E're I to thee, thou to thy self wast cruel.
Let weakness then with weakness come to parl
So near related, or the same of kind,

Thine forgive mine; that men may censure thine
The gentler, if severely thou exact not
More strength from me, then in thy self was found.
And what if Love, which thou interpret'st hate,
The jealousie of Love, powerful of sway
In human hearts, nor less in mine towards thee,
Caus'd what I did? I saw thee mutable
Of fancy, feard lest one day thou wouldst leave me
As her at Timna, sought by all means therefore
How to endear, and hold thee to me firmest:
No better way I saw then by importuning
To learn thy secrets, get into my power
Thy key of strength and safety: thou wilt say,
Why then reveal'd? I was assur'd by those
Who tempted me, that nothing was design'd
Against thee but safe custody, and hold:
That made for me, I knew that liberty
Would draw thee forth to perilous enterprises,
While I at home sate full of cares and fears
Wailing thy absence in my widow'd bed;
Here I should still enjoy thee day and night
Mine and Loves prisoner, not the Philistines,
Whole to my self, unhazarded abroad,
Fearless at home of partners in my love.
These reasons in Loves law have past for good,
Though fond and reasonless to some perhaps:
And Love hath oft, well meaning, wrought much wo,
Yet always pity or pardon hath obtain'd.
Be not unlike all others, not austere
As thou art strong, inflexible as steel.
If thou in strength all mortals dost exceed,
In uncompassionate anger do not so.

SAMSON
How cunningly the sorceress displays
Her own transgressions, to upbraid me mine!
That malice not repentance brought thee hither,
By this appears: I gave, thou say'st, th' example,
I led the way; bitter reproach, but true,
I to my self was false e're thou to me,
Such pardon therefore as I give my folly,
Take to thy wicked deed: which when thou seest
Impartial, self-severe, inexorable,
Thou wilt renounce thy seeking, and much rather
Confess it feign'd, weakness is thy excuse,
And I believe it, weakness to resist
Philistian gold: if weakness may excuse,
What Murtherer, what Traytor, Parricide,
Incestuous, Sacrilegious, but may plead it?
All wickedness is weakness: that plea therefore
With God or Man will gain thee no remission.

But Love constrain'd thee; call it furious rage
To satisfie thy lust: Love seeks to have Love;
My love how couldst thou hope, who tookst the way
To raise in me inexpiable hate,
Knowing, as needs I must, by thee betray'd?
In vain thou striv'st to cover shame with shame,
Or by evasions thy crime uncoverst more.

DALILA
Since thou determinst weakness for no plea
In man or woman, though to thy own condemning,
Hear what assaults I had, what snares besides,
What sieges girt me round, e're I consented;
Which might have aw'd the best resolv'd of men,
The constantest to have yielded without blame.
It was not gold, as to my charge thou lay'st,
That wrought with me: thou know'st the Magistrates
And Princes of my countrey came in person,
Sollicited, commanded, threatn'd, urg'd,
Adjur'd by all the bonds of civil Duty
And of Religion, press'd how just it was,
How honourable, how glorious to entrap
A common enemy, who had destroy'd
Such numbers of our Nation: and the Priest
Was not behind, but ever at my ear,
Preaching how meritorious with the gods
It would be to ensnare an irreligious
Dishonourer of Dagon: what had I
To oppose against such powerful arguments?
Only my love of thee held long debate;
And combated in silence all these reasons
With hard contest: at length that grounded maxim
So rife and celebrated in the mouths
Of wisest men; that to the public good
Private respects must yield; with grave authority'
Took full possession of me and prevail'd;
Vertue, as I thought, truth, duty so enjoyning.

SAMSON
I thought where all thy circling wiles would end;
In feign'd Religion, smooth hypocrisie.
But had thy love, still odiously pretended,
Bin, as it ought, sincere, it would have taught thee
Far other reasonings, brought forth other deeds.
I before all the daughters of my Tribe
And of my Nation chose thee from among
My enemies, lov'd thee, as too well thou knew'st,
Too well, unbosom'd all my secrets to thee,
Not out of levity, but over-powr'd
By thy request, who could deny thee nothing;
Yet now am judg'd an enemy. Why then

Didst thou at first receive me for thy husband?
Then, as since then, thy countries foe profest:
Being once a wife, for me thou wast to leave
Parents and countrey; nor was I their subject,
Nor under their protection but my own,
Thou mine, not theirs: if aught against my life
Thy countrey sought of thee, it sought unjustly,
Against the law of nature, law of nations,
No more thy countrey, but an impious crew
Of men conspiring to uphold thir state
By worse than hostile deeds, violating the ends
For which our countrey is a name so dear;
Not therefore to be obey'd. But zeal mov'd thee;
To please thy gods thou didst it; gods unable
To acquit themselves and prosecute their foes
But by ungodly deeds, the contradiction
Of their own deity, Gods cannot be:
Less therefore to be pleas'd, obey'd, or fear'd,
These false pretexts and varnish'd colours failing,
Bare in thy guilt how foul must thou appear?

DALILA
In argument with men a woman ever
Goes by the worse, whatever be her cause.

SAMSON
For want of words no doubt, or lack of breath,
Witness when I was worried with thy peals.

DALILA
I was a fool, too rash, and quite mistaken
In what I thought would have succeeded best.
Let me obtain forgiveness of thee, Samson,
Afford me place to shew what recompence
Towards thee I intend for what I have misdone,
Misguided: only what remains past cure
Bear not too sensibly, nor still insist
To afflict thy self in vain: though sight be lost,
Life yet hath many solaces, enjoy'd
Where other senses want not their delights
At home in leisure and domestic ease,
Exempt from many a care and chance to which
Eye-sight exposes daily men abroad.
I to the Lords will intercede, not doubting
Thir favourable ear, that I may fetch thee
From forth this loathsom prison-house, to abide
With me, where my redoubl'd love and care
With nursing diligence, to me glad office,
May ever tend about thee to old age
With all things grateful chear'd, and so suppli'd,
That what by me thou hast lost thou least shalt miss.

SAMSON

No, no, of my condition take no care;
It fits not; thou and I long since are twain;
Nor think me so unwary or accurst
To bring my feet again into the snare
Where once I have been caught; I know thy trains
Though dearly to my cost, thy ginns, and toyls;
Thy fair enchanted cup, and warbling charms
No more on me have power, their force is null'd,
So much of Adders wisdom I have learn't
To fence my ear against thy sorceries.
If in my flower of youth and strength, when all men
Lov'd, honour'd, fear'd me, thou alone could hate me
Thy Husband, slight me, sell me, and forgo me;
How wouldst thou use me now, blind, and thereby
Deceiveable, in most things as a child
Helpless, thence easily contemn'd, and scorn'd,
And last neglected? How wouldst thou insult
When I must live uxorious to thy will
In perfet thraldom, how again betray me,
Bearing my words and doings to the Lords
To gloss upon, and censuring, frown or smile?
This Gaol I count the house of Liberty
To thine whose doors my feet shall never enter.

DALILA

Let me approach at least, and touch thy hand.

SAMSON

Not for thy life, lest fierce remembrance wake
My sudden rage to tear thee joint by joint.
At distance I forgive thee, go with that;
Bewail thy falshood, and the pious works
It hath brought forth to make thee memorable
Among illustrious women, faithful wives:
Cherish thy hast'n'd widowhood with the gold
Of Matrimonial treason: so farewel.

DALILA

I see thou art implacable, more deaf
To prayers, then winds and seas, yet winds to seas
Are reconcil'd at length, and Sea to Shore:
Thy anger, unappeasable, still rages,
Eternal tempest never to be calm'd.
Why do I humble thus my self, and suing
For peace, reap nothing but repulse and hate?
Bid go with evil omen and the brand
Of infamy upon my name denounc't?
To mix with thy concernments I desist
Henceforth, nor too much disapprove my own.

Fame if not double-fac't is double-mouth'd,
And with contrary blast proclaims most deeds,
On both his wings, one black, th' other white,
Bears greatest names in his wild aerie flight.
My name perhaps among the Circumcis'd
In Dan, in Judah, and the bordering Tribes,
To all posterity may stand defam'd,
With malediction mention'd, and the blot
Of falshood most unconjugal traduc't.
But in my countrey where I most desire,
In Ecron, Gaza, Asdod, and in Gath
I shall be nam'd among the famousest
Of Women, sung at solemn festivals,
Living and dead recorded, who to save
Her countrey from a fierce destroyer, chose
Above the faith of wedlock-bands, my tomb
With odours visited and annual flowers.
Not less renown'd then in Mount Ephraim,
Jael who with inhospitable guile
Smote Sisera sleeping through the Temples nail'd.
Nor shall I count it hainous to enjoy
The public marks of honour and reward
Conferr'd upon me, for the piety
Which to my countrey I was judg'd to have shewn.
At this who ever envies or repines
I leave him to his lot, and like my own.

CHORUS
She's gone, a manifest Serpent by her sting
Discover'd in the end, till now conceal'd.

SAMSON
So let her go, God sent her to debase me,
And aggravate my folly who committed
To such a viper his most sacred trust
Of secresie, my safety, and my life.

CHORUS
Yet beauty, though injurious, hath strange power,
After offence returning, to regain
Love once possest, nor can be easily
Repuls't, without much inward passion felt
And secret sting of amorous remorse.

SAMSON
Love-quarrels oft in pleasing concord end,
Not wedlock-trechery endangering life.

CHORUS
It is not vertue, wisdom, valour, wit,
Strength, comliness of shape, or amplest merit

That womans love can win or long inherit;
But what it is, hard is to say,
Harder to hit,
(Which way soever men refer it)
Much like thy riddle, Samson, in one day
Or seven, though one should musing sit;
If any of these or all, the Timnian bride
Had not so soon preferr'd
Thy Paranymph, worthless to thee compar'd,
Successour in thy bed,
Nor both so loosly disally'd
Thir nuptials, nor this last so trecherously
Had shorn the fatal harvest of thy head.
Is it for that such outward ornament
Was lavish't on thir Sex, that inward gifts
Were left for hast unfinish't, judgment scant,
Capacity not rais'd to apprehend
Or value what is best
In choice, but oftest to affect the wrong?
Or was too much of self-love mixt,
Of constancy no root infixt,
That either they love nothing, or not long?
What e're it be, to wisest men and best
Seeming at first all heavenly under virgin veil,
Soft, modest, meek, demure,
Once join'd, the contrary she proves, a thorn
Intestin, far within defensive arms
A cleaving mischief, in his way to vertue
Adverse and turbulent, or by her charms
Draws him awry enslav'd
With dotage, and his sense deprav'd
To folly and shameful deeds which ruin ends.
What Pilot so expert but needs must wreck
Embarqu'd with such a Stears-mate at the Helm?
Favour'd of Heav'n who finds
One vertuous rarely found,
That in domestic good combines:
Happy that house! his way to peace is smooth:
But vertue which breaks through all opposition,
And all temptation can remove,
Most shines and most is acceptable above.
Therefore Gods universal Law
Gave to the man despotic power
Over his female in due awe,
Nor from that right to part an hour,
Smile she or lowre:
So shall he least confusion draw
On his whole life, not sway'd
By female usurpation, nor dismay'd.
But had we best retire, I see a storm?

SAMSON

Fair days have oft contracted wind and rain.

CHORUS

But this another kind of tempest brings.

SAMSON

Be less abstruse, my riddling days are past.

CHORUS

Look now for no inchanting voice, nor fear
The bait of honied words; a rougher tongue
Draws hitherward, I know him by his stride,
The Giant Harapha of Gath, his look
Haughty as is his pile high-built and proud.
Comes he in peace? what wind hath blown him hither
I less conjecture then when first I saw
The sumptuous Dalila floating this way:
His habit carries peace, his brow defiance.

SAMSON

Or peace or not, alike to me he comes.

CHORUS

His fraught we soon shall know, he now arrives.

HARAPHA

I come not Samson, to condole thy chance,
As these perhaps, yet wish it had not been,
Though for no friendly intent. I am of Gath,
Men call me Harapha, of stock renown'd
As Og or Anak and the Emims old
That Kiriathaim held, thou knowst me now
If thou at all art known. Much I have heard
Of thy prodigious might and feats perform'd
Incredible to me, in this displeas'd,
That I was never present on the place
Of those encounters, where we might have tri'd
Each others force in camp or listed field:
And now am come to see of whom such noise
Hath walk'd about, and each limb to survey,
If thy appearance answer loud report.

SAMSON

The way to know were not to see but taste.

HARAPHA

Dost thou already single me; I thought
Gives and the Mill had tam'd thee? O that fortune
Had brought me to the field where thou art fam'd
To have wrought such wonders with an Asses Jaw;

I should have forc'd thee soon with other arms,
Or left thy carkass where the Ass lay thrown:
So had the glory of Prowess been recover'd
To Palestine, won by a Philistine
From the unforeskinn'd race, of whom thou hear'st
The highest name for valiant Acts, that honour
Certain to have won by mortal duel from thee,
I lose, prevented by thy eyes put out.

SAMSON

Boast not of what thou wouldst have done, but do
What then thou would'st, thou seest it in thy hand.

HARAPHA

To combat with a blind man I disdain
And thou hast need much washing to be toucht.

SAMSON

Such usage as your honourable Lords
Afford me assassinated and betray'd,
Who durst not with thir whole united powers
In fight withstand me single and unarm'd,
Nor in the house with chamber Ambushes
Close-banded durst attaque me, no not sleeping,
Till they had hir'd a woman with their gold
Breaking her Marriage Faith to circumvent me.
Therefore without feign'd shifts let be assign'd
Some narrow place enclos'd, where sight may give thee.
Or rather flight, no great advantage on me;
Then put on all thy gorgeous arms, thy Helmet
And Brigandine of brass, thy broad Habergeon,
Vant-brass and Greves, and Gauntlet, add thy Spear
A Weavers beam, and seven-times-folded shield.
I only with an Oak'n staff will meet thee,
And raise such out-cries on thy clatter'd Iron,
Which long shall not with-hold mee from thy head,
That in a little time while breath remains thee,
Thou oft shalt wish thy self at Gath to boast
Again in safety what thou wouldst have done
To Samson, but shalt never see Gath more.

HARAPHA

Thou durst not thus disparage glorious arms
Which greatest Heroes have in battel worn,
Thir ornament and safety, had not spells
And black enchantments, some Magicians Art
Arm'd thee or charm'd thee strong, which thou from Heaven
Feigndst at thy birth was giv'n thee in thy hair,
Where strength can least abide, though all thy hairs
Were bristles rang'd like those that ridge the back
Of chaf't wild Boars, or ruffl'd Porcupines.

SAMSON

I know no Spells, use no forbidden Arts;
My trust is in the living God who gave me
At my Nativity this strength, diffus'd
No less through all my sinews, joints and bones,
Then thine, while I preserv'd these locks unshorn,
The pledge of my unviolated vow.
For proof hereof, if Dagon be thy god,
Go to his Temple, invocate his aid
With solemnest devotion, spread before him
How highly it concerns his glory now
To frustrate and dissolve these Magic spells,
Which I to be the power of Israel's God
Avow, and challenge Dagon to the test,
Offering to combat thee his Champion bold,
With th' utmost of his Godhead seconded:
Then thou shalt see, or rather to thy sorrow
Soon feel, whose God is strongest, thine or mine.

HARAPHA

Presume not on thy God, what e're he be,
Thee he regards not, owns not, hath cut off
Quite from his people, and delivered up
Into thy Enemies hand, permitted them
To put out both thine eyes, and fetter'd send thee
Into the common Prison, there to grind
Among the Slaves and Asses thy comrades,
As good for nothing else, no better service
With those, thy boyst'rous locks, no worthy match
For valour to assail, nor by the sword
Of noble Warriour, so to stain his honour,
But by the Barbers razor best subdu'd.

SAMSON

All these indignities, for such they are
From thine, these evils I deserve and more,
Acknowledge them from God inflicted on me
Justly, yet despair not of his final pardon
Whose ear is ever open; and his eye
Gracious to re-admit the suppliant;
In confidence whereof I once again
Defie thee to the trial of mortal fight,
By combat to decide whose god is God,
Thine or whom I with Israel's Sons adore.

HARAPHA

Fair honour that thou dost thy God, in trusting
He will accept thee to defend his cause,
A Murtherer, a Revolter, and a Robber.

SAMSON

Tongue-doubtie Giant, how dost thou prove me these?

HARAPHA

Is not thy Nation subject to our Lords?
Thir Magistrates confest it, when they took thee
As a League-breaker and deliver'd bound
Into our hands: for hadst thou not committed
Notorious murder on those thirty men
At Askalon, who never did thee harm,
Then like a Robber stripdst them of thir robes?
The Philistines, when thou hadst broke the league,
Went up with armed powers thee only seeking,
To others did no violence nor spoil.

SAMSON

Among the Daughters of the Philistines
I chose a Wife, which argu'd me no foe;
And in your City held my Nuptial Feast:
But your ill-meaning Politician Lords,
Under pretence of Bridal friends and guests,
Appointed to await me thirty spies,
Who threatning cruel death constrain'd the bride
To wring from me and tell to them my secret,
That solv'd the riddle which I had propos'd.
When I perceiv'd all set on enmity,
As on my enemies, where ever chanc'd,
I us'd hostility, and took thir spoil
To pay my underminers in thir coin.
My Nation was subjected to your Lords.
It was the force of Conquest; force with force
Is well ejected when the Conquer'd can.
But I a private person, whom my Countrey
As a league-breaker gave up bound, presum'd
Single Rebellion and did Hostile Acts.
I was no private but a person rais'd
With strength sufficient and command from Heav'n
To free my Countrey; if their servile minds
Me their Deliverer sent would not receive,
But to thir Masters gave me up for nought,
Th' unworthier they; whence to this day they serve.
I was to do my part from Heav'n assign'd,
And had perform'd it if my known offence
Had not disabl'd me, not all your force:
These shifts refuted, answer thy appellant
Though by his blindness maim'd for high attempts,
Who now defies thee thrice to single fight,
As a petty enterprise of small enforce.

HARAPHA

With thee a Man condemn'd, a Slave enrol'd,

Due by the Law to capital punishment?
To fight with thee no man of arms will deign.

SAMSON
Cam'st thou for this, vain boaster, to survey me,
To descant on my strength, and give thy verdict?
Come nearer, part not hence so slight inform'd;
But take good heed my hand survey not thee.
HARAPHA
O Baal-zebub! can my ears unus'd
Hear these dishonours, and not render death?

SAMSON
No man with-holds thee, nothing from thy hand
Fear I incurable; bring up thy van,
My heels are fetter'd, but my fist is free.

HARAPHA
This insolence other kind of answer fits.

SAMSON
Go baffl'd coward, lest I run upon thee,
Though in these chains, bulk without spirit vast,
And with one buffet lay thy structure low,
Or swing thee in the Air, then dash thee down
To the hazard of thy brains and shatter'd sides.

HARAPHA
By Astaroth e're long thou shalt lament
These braveries in Irons loaden on thee.

CHORUS
His Giantship is gone somewhat crestfall'n,
Stalking with less unconsci'nable strides,
And lower looks, but in a sultrie chafe.

SAMSON
I dread him not, nor all his Giant-brood,
Though Fame divulge him Father of five Sons
All of Gigantic size, Goliah chief.

CHORUS
He will directly to the Lords, I fear,
And with malitious counsel stir them up
Some way or other yet further to afflict thee.

SAMSON
He must allege some cause, and offer'd fight
Will not dare mention, lest a question rise
Whether he durst accept the offer or not,
And that he durst not plain enough appear'd.

Much more affliction then already felt
They cannot well impose, nor I sustain;
If they intend advantage of my labours
The work of many hands, which earns my keeping
With no small profit daily to my owners.
But come what will, my deadliest foe will prove
My speediest friend, by death to rid me hence,
The worst that he can give, to me the best.
Yet so it may fall out, because thir end
Is hate, not help to me, it may with mine
Draw thir own ruin who attempt the deed.

CHORUS
Oh how comely it is and how reviving
To the Spirits of just men long opprest!
When God into the hands of thir deliverer
Puts invincible might
To quell the mighty of the Earth, th' oppressour,
The brute and boist'rous force of violent men
Hardy and industrious to support
Tyrannic power, but raging to pursue
The righteous and all such as honour Truth;
He all thir Ammunition
And feats of War defeats
With plain Heroic magnitude of mind
And celestial vigour arm'd,
Thir Armories and Magazins contemns,
Renders them useless, while
With winged expedition
Swift as the lightning glance he executes
His errand on the wicked, who surpris'd
Lose thir defence distracted and amaz'd.
But patience is more oft the exercise
Of Saints, the trial of thir fortitude,
Making them each his own Deliverer,
And Victor over all
That tyrannie or fortune can inflict,
Either of these is in thy lot,
Samson, with might endu'd
Above the Sons of men; but sight bereav'd
May chance to number thee with those
Whom Patience finally must crown.
This Idols day hath bin to thee no day of rest,
Labouring thy mind
More then the working day thy hands,
And yet perhaps more trouble is behind.
For I descry this way
Some other tending, in his hand
A Scepter or quaint staff he bears,
Comes on amain, speed in his look.
By his habit I discern him now

A Publick Officer, and now at hand.
His message will be short and voluble.

PUBLICK OFFICER
Ebrews, the Pris'ner Samson here I seek.

CHORUS
His manacles remark him, there he sits.

PUBLICK OFFICER
Samson, to thee our Lords thus bid me say;
This day to Dagon is a solemn Feast,
With Sacrifices, Triumph, Pomp, and Games;
Thy strength they know surpassing human rate,
And now some public proof thereof require
To honour this great Feast, and great Assembly;
Rise therefore with all speed and come along,
Where I will see thee heartn'd and fresh clad
To appear as fits before th' illustrious Lords.

SAMSON
Thou knowst I am an Ebrew, therefore tell them,
Our Law forbids at thir Religious Rites
My presence; for that cause I cannot come.

PUBLICK OFFICER
This answer, be assur'd, will not content them.

SAMSON
Have they not Sword-players, and ev'ry sort
Of Gymnic Artists, Wrestlers, Riders, Runners,
Juglers and Dancers, Antics, Mummers, Mimics,
But they must pick me out with shackles tir'd,
And over-labour'd at thir publick Mill,
To make them sport with blind activity?
Do they not seek occasion of new quarrels
On my refusal to distress me more,
Or make a game of my calamities?
Return the way thou cam'st, I will not come.

PUBLICK OFFICER
Regard thy self, this will offend them highly.

Sam: My self? my conscience and internal peace.
Can they think me so broken, so debas'd
With corporal servitude, that my mind ever
Will condescend to such absurd commands?
Although thir drudge, to be thir fool or jester,
And in my midst of sorrow and heart-grief
To shew them feats, and play before thir god,
The worst of all indignities, yet on me

Joyn'd with extream contempt? I will not come.

PUBLICK OFFICER
My message was impos'd on me with speed,
Brooks no delay: is this thy resolution?

SAMSON
So take it with what speed thy message needs.

PUBLICK OFFICER
I am sorry what this stoutness will produce.

SAMSON
Perhaps thou shalt have cause to sorrow indeed.

CHORUS
Consider, Samson; matters now are strain'd
Up to the highth, whether to bold or break;
He's gone, and who knows how he may report
Thy words by adding fuel to the flame?
Expect another message more imperious,
More Lordly thund'ring then thou well wilt bear.

SAMSON
Shall I abuse this Consecrated gift
Of strength, again returning with my hair
After my great transgression, so requite
Favour renew'd, and add a greater sin
By prostituting holy things to Idols;
A Nazarite in place abominable
Vaunting my strength in honour to thir Dagon?
Besides, how vile, contemptible, ridiculous,
What act more execrably unclean, prophane?

CHORUS
Yet with this strength thou serv'st the Philistines,
Idolatrous, uncircumcis'd, unclean.

SAMSON
Not in thir Idol-worship, but by labour
Honest and lawful to deserve my food
Of those who have me in thir civil power.

CHORUS
Where the heart joins not, outward acts defile not

SAMSON
Where outward force constrains, the sentence holds:
But who constrains me to the Temple of Dagon,
Not dragging? the Philistian Lords command.
Commands are no constraints. If I obey them,

I do it freely; venturing to displease
God for the fear of Man, and Man prefer,
Set God behind: which in his jealousie
Shall never, unrepented, find forgiveness.
Yet that he may dispense with me or thee
Present in Temples at Idolatrous Rites
For some important cause, thou needst not doubt.

CHORUS
How thou wilt here come off surmounts my reach.

SAMSON
Be of good courage, I begin to feel
Some rouzing motions in me which dispose
To something extraordinary my thoughts.
I with this Messenger will go along,
Nothing to do, be sure, that may dishonour
Our Law, or stain my vow of Nazarite.
If there be aught of presage in the mind,
This day will be remarkable in my life
By some great act, or of my days the last.

CHORUS
In time thou hast resolv'd, the man returns.

PUBLICK OFFICER
Samson, this second message from our Lords
To thee I am bid say. Art thou our Slave,
Our Captive, at the public Mill our drudge,
And dar'st thou at our sending and command
Dispute thy coming? come without delay;
Or we shall find such Engines to assail
And hamper thee, as thou shalt come of force,
Though thou wert firmlier fastn'd then a rock.

SAMSON
I could be well content to try thir Art,
Which to no few of them would prove pernicious.
Yet knowing thir advantages too many,
Because they shall not trail me through thir streets
Like a wild Beast, I am content to go.
Masters commands come with a power resistless
To such as owe them absolute subjection;
And for a life who will not change his purpose?
(So mutable are all the ways of men)
Yet this be sure, in nothing to comply
Scandalous or forbidden in our Law.

PUBLICK OFFICER
I praise thy resolution, doff these links:
By this compliance thou wilt win the Lords

To favour, and perhaps to set thee free.

SAMSON

Brethren farewel, your company along
I will not wish, lest it perhaps offend them
To see me girt with Friends; and how the sight
Of me as of a common Enemy,
So dreaded once, may now exasperate them
I know not. Lords are Lordliest in thir wine,
And the well-feasted Priest then soonest fir'd
With zeal, if aught Religion seem concern'd:
No less the people on thir Holy-days
Impetuous, insolent, unquenchable;
Happ'n what may, of me expect to hear
Nothing dishonourable, impure, unworthy
Our God, our Law, my Nation, or my self,
The last of me or no I cannot warrant.

CHORUS

Go, and the Holy One
Of Israel be thy guide
To what may serve his glory best, & spread his name
Great among the Heathen round:
Send thee the Angel of thy Birth, to stand
Fast by thy side, who from thy Fathers field
Rode up in flames after his message told
Of thy conception, and be now a shield
Of fire; that Spirit that first rusht on thee
In the camp of Dan
Be efficacious in thee now at need.
For never was from Heaven imparted
Measure of strength so great to mortal seed,
As in thy wond'rous actions Hath been seen.
But wherefore comes old Manoa in such hast
With youthful steps? much livelier than e're while
He seems: supposing here to find his Son,
Or of him bringing to us some glad news?

MANOA

Peace with you brethren; my inducement hither
Was not at present here to find my Son,
By order of the Lords new parted hence
To come and play before them at thir Feast.
I heard all as I came, the City rings
And numbers thither flock, I had no will,
Lest I should see him forc't to things unseemly.
But that which moved my coming now, was chiefly
To give ye part with me what hope I have
With good success to work his liberty.

CHORUS

That hope would much rejoyce us to partake
With thee; say reverend Sire, we thirst to hear.

MANOA

I have attempted one by one the Lords
Either at home, or through the high street passing,
With supplication prone and Fathers tears
To accept of ransom for my Son thir pris'ner,
Some much averse I found and wondrous harsh,
Contemptuous, proud, set on revenge and spite;
That part most reverenc'd Dagon and his Priests,
Others more moderate seeming, but thir aim
Private reward, for which both God and State
They easily would set to sale, a third
More generous far and civil, who confess'd
They had anough reveng'd, having reduc't
Thir foe to misery beneath thir fears,
The rest was magnanimity to remit,
If some convenient ransom were propos'd.
What noise or shout was that? it tore the Skie.

CHORUS

Doubtless the people shouting to behold
Thir once great dread, captive, & blind before them,
Or at some proof of strength before them shown.

MANOA

His ransom, if my whole inheritance
May compass it, shall willingly be paid
And numberd down: much rather I shall chuse
To live the poorest in my Tribe, then richest,
And he in that calamitous prison left.
No, I am fixt not to part hence without him.
For his redemption all my Patrimony,
If need be, I am ready to forgo
And quit: not wanting him, I shall want nothing.

CHORUS

Fathers are wont to lay up for thir Sons,
Thou for thy Son art bent to lay out all;
Sons wont to nurse thir Parents in old age,
Thou in old age car'st how to nurse thy Son,
Made older then thy age through eye-sight lost.

MANOA

It shall be my delight to tend his eyes,
And view him sitting in the house, enobl'd
With all those high exploits by him atchiev'd,
And on his shoulders waving down those locks,
That of a Nation arm'd the strength contain'd:
And I perswade me God had not permitted

His strength again to grow up with his hair
Garrison'd round about him like a Camp
Of faithful Souldiery, were not his purpose
To use him further yet in some great service,
Not to sit idle with so great a gift
Useless, and thence ridiculous about him.
And since his strength with eye-sight was not lost,
God will restore him eye-sight to his strength.

CHORUS
Thy hopes are not ill founded nor seem vain
Of his delivery, and thy joy thereon
Conceiv'd, agreeable to a Fathers love,
In both which we, as next participate.

MANOA
I know your friendly minds and O what noise!
Mercy of Heav'n what hideous noise was that!
Horribly loud unlike the former shout.

CHORUS
Noise call you it or universal groan
As if the whole inhabitation perish'd,
Blood, death, and deathful deeds are in that noise,
Ruin, destruction at the utmost point.

MANOA
Of ruin indeed methought I heard the noise,
Oh it continues, they have slain my Son.

CHORUS
Thy Son is rather slaying them, that outcry
From slaughter of one foe could not ascend.

MANOA
Some dismal accident it needs must be;
What shall we do, stay here or run and see?

CHORUS
Best keep together here, lest running thither
We unawares run into dangers mouth.
This evil on the Philistines is fall'n
From whom could else a general cry be heard?
The sufferers then will scarce molest us here,
From other hands we need not much to fear.
What if his eye-sight (for to Israels God
Nothing is hard) by miracle restor'd,
He now be dealing dole among his foes,
And over heaps of slaughter'd walk his way?

MANOA

That were a joy presumptuous to be thought.

CHORUS
Yet God hath wrought things as incredible
For his people of old; what hinders now?

MANOA
He can I know, but doubt to think be will;
Yet Hope would fain subscribe, and tempts Belief.
A little stay will bring some notice hither.

CHORUS
Of good or bad so great, of bad the sooner;
For evil news rides post, while good news baits.
And to our wish I see one hither speeding,
An Ebrew, as I guess, and of our Tribe.

MESSENGER
O whither shall I run, or which way flie
The sight of this so horrid spectacle
Which earst my eyes beheld and yet behold;
For dire imagination still persues me.
But providence or instinct of nature seems,
Or reason though disturb'd, and scarse consulted
To have guided me aright, I know not how,
To thee first reverend Manoa, and to these
My Countreymen, whom here I knew remaining,
As at some distance from the place of horrour,
So in the sad event too much concern'd.

MANOA
The accident was loud, & here before thee
With rueful cry, yet what it was we hear not,
No Preface needs, thou seest we long to know.

MESSENGER
It would burst forth, but I recover breath
And sense distract, to know well what I utter.

MANOA
Tell us the sum, the circumstance defer.

MESSENGER
Gaza yet stands, but all her Sons are fall'n,
All in a moment overwhelm'd and fall'n.

MANOA
Sad, but thou knowst to Israelites not saddest
The desolation of a Hostile City.

MESSENGER

Feed on that first, there may in grief be surfet.

MANOA
Relate by whom.

MESSENGER
By Samson.

MANOA
That still lessens
The sorrow, and converts it nigh to joy.

MESSENGER
Ah Manoa I refrain, too suddenly
To utter what will come at last too soon;
Lest evil tidings with too rude irruption
Hitting thy aged ear should pierce too deep.

MANOA
Suspense in news is torture, speak them out.

MESSENGER
Then take the worst in brief, Samson is dead.

MANOA
The worst indeed, O all my hope's defeated
To free him hence! but death who sets all free
Hath paid his ransom now and full discharge.
What windy joy this day had I conceiv'd
Hopeful of his Delivery, which now proves
Abortive as the first-born bloom of spring
Nipt with the lagging rear of winters frost.
Yet e're I give the rains to grief, say first,
How dy'd he? death to life is crown or shame.
All by him fell thou say'st, by whom fell he,
What glorious band gave Samson his deaths wound?

MESSENGER
Unwounded of his enemies he fell.

MANOA
Wearied with slaughter then or how? explain.

MESSENGER
By his own hands.

MANOA
Self-violence? what cause
Brought him so soon at variance with himself
Among his foes?

MESSENGER

Inevitable cause
At once both to destroy and be destroy'd;
The Edifice where all were met to see him
Upon thir heads and on his own he pull'd.

MANOA

O lastly over-strong against thy self!
A dreadful way thou took'st to thy revenge.
More than anough we know; but while things yet
Are in confusion, give us if thou canst,
Eye-witness of what first or last was done,
Relation more particular and distinct.

MESSENGER

Occasions drew me early to this City,
And as the gates I enter'd with Sun-rise,
The morning Trumpets Festival proclaim'd
Through each high street: little I had dispatch't
When all abroad was rumour'd that this day
Samson should be brought forth to shew the people
Proof of his mighty strength in feats and games;
I sorrow'd at his captive state, but minded
Not to be absent at that spectacle.
The building was a spacious Theatre
Half round on two main Pillars vaulted high,
With seats where all the Lords and each degree
Of sort, might sit in order to behold,
The other side was op'n, where the throng
On banks and scaffolds under Skie might stand;
I among these aloof obscurely stood.
The Feast and noon grew high, and Sacrifice
Had fill'd thir hearts with mirth, high chear, & wine,
When to thir sports they turn'd. Immediately
Was Samson as a public servant brought,
In thir state Livery clad; before him Pipes
And Timbrels, on each side went armed guards,
Both horse and foot before him and behind
Archers, and Slingers, Cataphracts and Spears.
At sight of him the people with a shout
Rifted the Air clamouring thir god with praise,
Who had made thir dreadful enemy thir thrall.
He patient but undaunted where they led him.
Came to the place, and what was set before him
Which without help of eye, might be assay'd,
To heave, pull, draw, or break, he still perform'd
All with incredible, stupendious force,
None daring to appear Antagonist.
At length for intermission sake they led him
Between the pillars; he his guide requested
(For so from such as nearer stood we heard)

As over-tir'd to let him lean a while
With both his arms on those two massie Pillars
That to the arched roof gave main support.
He unsuspitious led him; which when Samson
Felt in his arms, with head a while enclin'd,
And eyes fast fixt he stood, as one who pray'd,
Or some great matter in his mind revolv'd.
At last with head erect thus cryed aloud,
Hitherto, Lords, what your commands impos'd
I have perform'd, as reason was, obeying,
Not without wonder or delight beheld.
Now of my own accord such other tryal
I mean to shew you of my strength, yet greater;
As with amaze shall strike all who behold.
This utter'd, straining all his nerves he bow'd,
As with the force of winds and waters pent,
When Mountains tremble, those two massie Pillars
With horrible convulsion to and fro,
He tugg'd, he shook, till down they came and drew
The whole roof after them, with burst of thunder
Upon the heads of all who sate beneath,
Lords, Ladies, Captains, Councellors, or Priests,
Thir choice nobility and flower, not only
Of this but each Philistian City round
Met from all parts to solemnize this Feast.
Samson with these immixt, inevitably
Pulld down the same destruction on himself;
The vulgar only scap'd who stood without.

CHORUS
O dearly-bought revenge, yet glorious!
Living or dying thou hast fulfill'd
The work for which thou wast foretold
To Israel and now ly'st victorious
Among thy slain self-kill'd
Not willingly, but tangl'd in the fold
Of dire necessity, whose law in death conjoin'd
Thee with thy slaughter'd foes in number more
Then all thy life had slain before.

SEMI-CHORUS
While thir hearts were jocund and sublime
Drunk with Idolatry, drunk with Wine,
And fat regorg'd of Bulls and Goats,
Chaunting thir Idol, and preferring
Before our living Dread who dwells
In Silo his bright Sanctuary:
Among them he a spirit of phrenzie sent,
Who hurt thir minds,
And urg'd them on with mad desire
To call in hast for thir destroyer;

They only set on sport and play
Unweetingly importun'd
Thir own destruction to come speedy upon them.
So fond are mortal men
Fall'n into wrath divine,
As thir own ruin on themselves to invite,
Insensate left, or to sense reprobate,
And with blindness internal struck.

SEMI-CHORUS
But he though blind of sight,
Despis'd and thought extinguish't quite,
With inward eyes illuminated
His fierie vertue rouz'd
From under ashes into sudden flame,
And as an ev'ning Dragon came,
Assailant on the perched roosts,
And nests in order rang'd
Of tame villatic Fowl; but as an Eagle
His cloudless thunder bolted on thir heads.
So vertue giv'n for lost,
Deprest, and overthrown, as seem'd,
Like that self-begott'n bird
In the Arabian woods embost,
That no second knows nor third,
And lay e're while a Holocaust,
From out her ashie womb now teem'd
Revives, reflourishes, then vigorous most
When most unactive deem'd,
And though her body die, her fame survives,
A secular bird ages of lives.

MANOA
Come, come, no time for lamentation now,
Nor much more cause, Samson hath quit himself
Like Samson, and heroicly hath finish'd
A life Heroic, on his Enemies
Fully reveng'd, hath left them years of mourning,
And lamentation to the Sons of Caphtor
Through all Philistian bounds. To Israel
Honour hath left, and freedom, let but them
Find courage to lay hold on this occasion,
To himself and Fathers house eternal fame;
And which is best and happiest yet, all this
With God not parted from him, as was feard,
But favouring and assisting to the end.
Nothing is here for tears, nothing to wail
Or knock the breast, no weakness, no contempt,
Dispraise, or blame, nothing but well and fair,
And what may quiet us in a death so noble.
Let us go find the body where it lies

Sok't in his enemies blood, and from the stream
With lavers pure and cleansing herbs wash off
The clotted gore. I with what speed the while
(Gaza is not in plight to say us nay)
Will send for all my kindred, all my friends
To fetch him hence and solemnly attend
With silent obsequie and funeral train
Home to his Fathers house: there will I build him
A Monument, and plant it round with shade
Of Laurel ever green, and branching Palm,
With all his Trophies hung, and Acts enroll'd
In copious Legend, or sweet Lyric Song.
Thither shall all the valiant youth resort,
And from his memory inflame thir breasts
To matchless valour, and adventures high:
The Virgins also shall on feastful days
Visit his Tomb with flowers, only bewailing
His lot unfortunate in nuptial choice,
From whence captivity and loss of eyes.

CHORUS
All is best, though we oft doubt,
What th' unsearchable dispose
Of highest wisdom brings about,
And ever best found in the close.
Oft he seems to hide his face,
But unexpectedly returns
And to his faithful Champion hath in place
Bore witness gloriously; whence Gaza mourns
And all that band them to resist
His uncontroulable intent,
His servants he with new acquist
Of true experience from this great event
With peace and consolation hath dismist,
And calm of mind all passion spent.

LYCIDAS

In this Monody the Author bewails a learned Friend, unfortunatly drown'd in his Passage from
Chester on the Irish Seas. And by occasion foretels the ruine of our corrupted Clergy then in their
height.

Yet once more, O ye Laurels, and once more
Ye Myrtles brown, with Ivy never-sear,
I com to pluck your Berries harsh and crude,
And with forc'd fingers rude,
Shatter your leaves before the mellowing year.
Bitter constraint, and sad occasion dear,

Compels me to disturb your season due:
For Lycidas is dead, dead ere his prime
Young Lycidas, and hath not left his peer:
Who would not sing for Lycidas? he knew
Himself to sing, and build the lofty rhyme.
He must not flote upon his watry bear
Unwept, and welter to the parching wind,
Without the meed of som melodious tear.

Begin then, Sisters of the sacred well,
That from beneath the seat of Jove doth spring,
Begin, and somwhat loudly sweep the string.
Hence with denial vain, and coy excuse,
So may som gentle Muse
With lucky words favour my destin'd Urn,
And as he passes turn,
And bid fair peace be to my sable shrowd.
For we were nurst upon the self-same hill,
Fed the same flock by fountain, shade, and rill.

Together both, ere the high Lawns appear'd
Under the opening eye-lids of the morn,
We drove a field and both together heard
What time the Gray-fly winds her sultry horn,
Batt'ning our flocks with the fresh dews of night,
Oft till the Star that rose, at Ev'ning, bright
Toward Heav'ns descent had slop'd his westering wheel.
Mean while the Rural ditties were not mute,
Temper'd to th'Oaten Flute;
Rough Satyrs danc'd, and Fauns with clov'n heel,
From the glad sound would not be absent long,
And old Damoetas lov'd to hear our song.

But O the heavy change, now thou art gon,
Now thou art gon, and never must return!
Thee Shepherd, thee the Woods, and desert Caves,
With wilde Thyme and the gadding Vine o'regrown,
And all their echoes mourn.
The Willows, and the Hazle Copses green,
Shall now no more be seen,
Fanning their joyous Leaves to thy soft layes.
As killing as the Canker to the Rose,
Or Taint-worm to the weanling Herds that graze,
Or Frost to Flowers, that their gay wardrop wear,
When first the White thorn blows;
Such, Lycidas, thy loss to Shepherds ear.

Where were ye Nymphs when the remorseless deep
Clos'd o're the head of your lov'd Lycidas?
For neither were ye playing on the steep,
Where your old Bards, the famous Druids ly,

Nor on the shaggy top of Mona high,
Nor yet where Deva spreads her wisard stream:
Ay me, I fondly dream!
Had ye bin there -- for what could that have don?
What could the Muse her self that Orpheus bore,
The Muse her self, for her inchanting son
Whom Universal nature did lament,
When by the rout that made the hideous roar,
His goary visage down the stream was sent,
Down the swift Hebrus to the Lesbian shore.

Alas! What boots it with uncessant care
To tend the homely slighted Shepherds trade,
And strictly meditate the thankles Muse,
Were it not better don as others use,
To sport with Amaryllis in the shade,
Or with the tangles of Neaera's hair?
Fame is the spur that the clear spirit doth raise
(That last infirmity of Noble mind)
To scorn delights, and live laborious dayes:
But the fair Guerdon when we hope to find,
And think to burst out into sudden blaze.
Comes the blind Fury with th'abhorred shears,
And slits the thin spun life. But not the praise,
Phoebus repli'd, and touch'd my trembling ears;
Fame is no plant that grows on mortal soil,
Nor in the glistering foil
Set off to th'world, nor in broad rumour lies,
But lives and spreds aloft by those pure eyes,
And perfet witnes of all judging Jove;
As he pronounces lastly on each deed,
Of so much fame in Heav'n expect thy meed.

O Fountain Arethuse, and thou honour'd floud,
Smooth-sliding Mincius, crown'd with vocall reeds,
That strain I heard was of a higher mood:
But now my Oate proceeds,
And listens to the Herald of the Sea
That came in Neptune's plea,
He ask'd the Waves, and ask'd the Fellon winds,
What hard mishap hath doom'd this gentle swain?
And question'd every gust of rugged wings
That blows from off each beaked Promontory,
They knew not of his story,
And sage Hippotades their answer brings,
That not a blast was from his dungeon stray'd,
The Ayr was calm, and on the level brine,
Sleek Panope with all her sisters play'd.
It was that fatall and perfidious Bark
Built in th'eclipse, and rigg'd with curses dark,
That sunk so low that sacred head of thine.

Next Camus, reverend Sire, went footing slow,
His Mantle hairy, and his Bonnet sedge,
Inwrought with figures dim, and on the edge
Like to that sanguine flower inscrib'd with woe.
Ah; Who hath reft (quoth he) my dearest pledge?
Last came, and last did go,
The Pilot of the Galilean lake,
Two massy Keyes he bore of metals twain,
(The Golden opes, the Iron shuts amain)
He shook his Miter'd locks, and stern bespake,
How well could I have spar'd for thee, young swain,
Anow of such as for their bellies sake,
Creep and intrude, and climb into the fold?
Of other care they little reck'ning make,
Then how to scramble at the shearers feast,
And shove away the worthy bidden guest.
Blind mouthes! that scarce themselves know how to hold
A Sheep-hook, or have learn'd ought els the least
That to the faithfull Herdmans art belongs!
What recks it them? What need they? They are sped;
And when they list, their lean and flashy songs
Grate on their scrannel Pipes of wretched straw,
The hungry Sheep look up, and are not fed,
But swoln with wind, and the rank mist they draw,
Rot inwardly, and foul contagion spread:
Besides what the grim Woolf with privy paw
Daily devours apace, and nothing sed,
But that two-handed engine at the door,
Stands ready to smite once, and smite no more.

Return Alpheus, the dread voice is past,
That shrunk thy streams; Return Sicilian Muse,
And call the Vales, and bid them hither cast
Their Bels, and Flourets of a thousand hues.
Ye valleys low where the milde whispers use,
Of shades and wanton winds, and gushing brooks,
On whose fresh lap the swart Star sparely looks,
Throw hither all your quaint enameld eyes,
That on the green terf suck the honied showres,
And purple all the ground with vernal flowres.
Bring the rathe Primrose that forsaken dies.
The tufted Crow-toe, and pale Gessamine,
The white Pink, and the Pansie freakt with jeat,
The glowing Violet.
The Musk-rose, and the well attir'd Woodbine.
With Cowslips wan that hang the pensive hed,
And every flower that sad embroidery wears:
Bid Amaranthus all his beauty shed,
Daffadillies fill their cups with tears,
And strew the Laureat Herse where Lycid lies.

For so to interpose a little ease,
Let our frail thoughts dally with false surmise.
Ah me! Whilst thee the shores, and sounding Seas
Wash far away, where ere thy bones are hurl'd
Whether beyond the stormy Hebrides.
Where thou perhaps under the whelming tide
Visit'st the bottom of the monstrous world;
Or whether thou to our moist vows deny'd,
Sleep'st by the fable of Bellerus old,
Where the great vision of the guarded Mount
Looks toward Namancos and Bayona's hold;
Look homeward Angel now, and melt with ruth.
And, O ye Dolphins, waft the haples youth.

Weep no more, woful Shepherds weep no more,
For Lycidas your sorrow is not dead,
Sunk though he be beneath the watry floar,
So sinks the day-star in the Ocean bed,
And yet anon repairs his drooping head,
And tricks his beams, and with new spangled Ore,
Flames in the forehead of the morning sky:
So Lycidas sunk low, but mounted high,
Through the dear might of him that walk'd the waves
Where other groves, and other streams along,
With Nectar pure his oozy Lock's he laves,
And hears the unexpressive nuptiall Song,
In the blest Kingdoms meek of joy and love.
There entertain him all the Saints above,
In solemn troops, and sweet Societies
That sing, and singing in their glory move,
And wipe the tears for ever from his eyes.
Now Lycidas the Shepherds weep no more;
Hence forth thou art the Genius of the shore,
In thy large recompense and shalt be good
To all that wander in that perilous flood.

Thus sang the uncouth Swain to th'Okes and rills,
While the still morn went out with Sandals gray,
He touch'd the tender stops of various Quills,
With eager thought warbling his Dorick lay:
And now the Sun had stretch'd out all the hills,
And now was dropt into the Western bay;
At last he rose, and twitch'd his Mantle blew:
To morrow to fresh Woods, and Pastures new.

To the Right Honourable, John Lord Vicount Bracly, Son and Heir apparent to the Earl of
Bridgewater, &c.

My LORD,

This Poem, which receiv'd its first occasion of Birth from your Self, and others of your Noble Family, and much honour from your own Person in the performance, now returns again to make a finall Dedication of it self to you. Although not openly acknowledg'd by the Author, yet it is a legitimate off-spring, so lovely, and so much desired, that the often Copying of it hath tired my Pen to give my several friends satisfaction, and brought me to a necessity of producing it to the publike view; and now to offer it up in all rightfull devotion to those fair Hopes, and rare endowments of your much-promising Youth, which give a full assurance, to all that know you, of a future excellence. Live sweet Lord to be the honour of your Name, and receive this as your own, from the hands of him, who hath by many favours been long oblig'd to your most honour'd Parents, and as in this representation your attendant Thyrsis, so now in all reall expression

Your faithfull, and most humble Servant

H. LAWES.

The Copy of a Letter writt'n by Sir HENRY WOOTTON, to the Author, upon the following Poem.

From the Colledge, this day of April.

SIR,
It was a special favour, when you lately bestowed upon me here, the first taste of your acquaintance, though no longer then to make me know that I wanted more time to value it, and to enjoy it rightly; and in truth, if I could then have imagined your farther stay in these parts, which I understood afterwards by Mr. H. I would have been bold in our vulgar phrase to mend my draught (for you left me with an extreme thirst) and to have begged your conversation again, joyntly with your said learned Friend, at a poor meal or two, that we might have banded together som good Authors of the antient time: Among which, I observed you to have been familiar.

Since your going, you have charg'd me with new Obligations, both for a very kinde Letter from you dated the sixth of this Month, and for a dainty peece of entertainment which came therwith. Wherin I should much commend the Tragical part, if the Lyrical did not ravish me with a certain Dorique delicacy in your Songs and Odes, wherunto I must plainly confess to have seen yet nothing parallel in our Language: Ipsa mollities. But I must not omit to tell you, that I now onely owe you thanks for intimating unto me (how modestly soever) the true Artificer. For the work it self I had view'd som good while before, with singular delight, having receiv'd it from our common Friend Mr. R. in the very close of the late R's Poems, Printed at Oxford, wherunto it was added (as I now suppose) that the Accessory might help out the Principal, according to the Art of Stationers, and to leave the Reader Con la bocca dolce.

Now Sir, concerning your travels, wherin I may challenge a little more priviledge of Discours with you; I suppose you will not blanch Paris in your way; therfore I have been bold to trouble you with a few lines to Mr. M. B. whom you shall easily find attending the young Lord S. as his Governour, and you may surely receive from him good directions for the shaping of your farther journey into Italy, where he did reside by my choice som time for the King, after mine own recess from Venice.

I should think that your best Line will be thorow the whole length of France to Marseilles, and thence by Sea to Genoa, whence the passage into Tuscany is as Diurnal as a Gravesend Barge: I hasten as you do to Florence, or Siena, the rather tell you a short story from the interest you have given me in your safety.

At Siena I was tabled in the House of one Alberto Scipioni, an old Roman Courtier in dangerous times, having bin Steward to the Duca di Pagliano, who with all his Family were strangled save this onely man that escap'd by foresight of the Tempest: With him I had often much chat of those affairs; Into which he took pleasure to look back from his Native Harbour: and at my departure toward Rome (which had been the center of his experience) I had wonn confidence enough to beg his advice, how I might carry my self securely there, without offence of mine own conscience. Signor Arrigo mio (sayes he) I pensieri stretti, & il viso sciolto, will go safely over the whole World: Of which Delphian Oracle (for so I have found it) your judgement doth need no commentary; and therfore (Sir) I will commit you with it to the best of all securities, Gods dear love, remaining

Your Friend as much at command as any of longer date,

Henry Wootton.

Postscript.

SIR, I have expressly sent this my Foot-boy to prevent your departure without som acknowledgement from me of the receipt of your obliging Letter, having myself through som busines, I know not how, neglected the ordinary conveyance. In any part where I shall understand you fixed, I shall be glad, and diligent to entertain you with Home-Novelties; even for som fomentation of our friendship, too soon interrupted in the Cradle.

THE PERSONS

The attendant Spirit afterwards in the habit of Thyrsis.
Comus with his crew.
The Lady.
Elder Brother.
Younger Brother.
Sabrina the Nymph.

The cheif persons which presented, were
The Lord Bracly.
Mr. Thomas Egerton his Brother,
The Lady Alice Egerton.

THE FIRST SCENE DISCOVERS A WILDE WOOD

The attendant **SPIRIT** descends or enters.

SPIRIT
Before the starry threshold of Joves Court
My mansion is, where those immortal shapes

Of bright aereal Spirits live insphear'd
In Regions milde of calm and serene Ayr,
Above the smoak and stirr of this dim spot,
Which men call Earth, and with low-thoughted care
Confin'd, and pester'd in this pin-fold here,
Strive to keep up a frail, and Feaverish being
Unmindfull of the crown that Vertue gives
After this mortal change, to her true Servants
Amongst the enthron'd gods on Sainted seats.
Yet som there he that by due steps aspire
To lay their just hands on that Golden Key
That ope's the Palace of Eternity:
To such my errand is, and but for such,
I would not soil these pure Ambrosial weeds,
With the rank vapours of this Sin-worn mould.
But to my task. Neptune besides the sway
Of every salt Flood, and each ebbing Stream,
Took in by lot 'twixt high, and neather Jove,
Imperial rule of all the Sea-girt Iles
That like to rich, and various gemms inlay
The unadorned boosom of the Deep,
Which he to grace his tributary gods
By course commits to severall government,
And gives them leave to wear their Saphire crowns,
And weild their little tridents, but this Ile
The greatest, and the best of all the main
He quarters to his blu-hair'd deities,
And all this tract that fronts the falling Sun
A noble Peer of mickle trust, and power
Has in his charge, with temper'd awe to guide
An old, and haughty Nation proud in Arms:
Where his fair off-spring nurs't in Princely lore,
Are coming to attend their Fathers state,
And new-entrusted Scepter, but their way
Lies through the perplex't paths of this drear Wood,
The nodding horror of whose shady brows
Threats the forlorn and wandring Passinger.
And here their tender age might suffer perill,
But that by quick command from Soveran Jove
I was dispatcht for their defence, and guard;
And listen why, for I will tell ye now
What never yet was heard in Tale or Song
From old, or modern Bard in Hall, or Bowr.
Bacchus that first from out the purple Grape,
Crush't the sweet poyson of mis-used Wine
After the Tuscan Mariners transform'd
Coasting the Tyrrhene shore, as the winds listed,
On Circes Hand fell (who knows not Circe
The daughter of the Sun? Whose charmed Cup
Whoever tasted, lost his upright shape,
And downward fell into a groveling Swine)

This Nymph that gaz'd upon his clustring locks,
With Ivy berries wreath'd, and his blithe youth,
Had by him, ere he parted thence, a Son
Much like his Father, but his Mother more,
Whom therfore she brought up and Comus named,
Who ripe, and frolick of his full grown age,
Roving the Celtic, and Iberian fields,
At last betakes him to this ominous Wood,
And in thick shelter of black shades imbowr'd,
Excells his Mother at her mighty Art,
Offring to every weary Travailer,
His orient liquor in a Crystal Glasse,
To quench the drouth of Phoebus, which as they taste
(For most do taste through fond intemperate thirst)
Soon as the Potion works, their human count'nance,
Th' express resemblance of the gods, is chang'd
Into som brutish form of Woolf, or Bear,
Or Ounce, or Tiger, Hog, or bearded Goat,
All other parts remaining as they were,
And they, so perfect is their misery,
Not once perceive their foul disfigurement,
But boast themselves more comely then before
And all their friends, and native home forget
To roule with pleasure in a sensual stie.
Therfore when any favour'd of high Jove,
Chances to pass through this adventrous glade,
Swift as the Sparkle of a glancing Star,
I shoot from Heav'n to give him safe convoy,
As now I do: But first I must put off
These my skie robes spun out of Iris Wooff,
And take the Weeds and likenes of a Swain,
That to the service of this house belongs,
Who with his soft Pipe, and smooth-dittied Song,
Well knows to still the wilde winds when they roar,
And hush the waving Woods, nor of lesse faith,
And in this office of his Mountain watch,
Likeliest, and neerest to the present ayd
Of this occasion. But I hear the tread
Of hatefull steps, I must be viewles now.

COMUS enters with a Charming Rod in one hand, his Glass in the other, with him a rout of monsters, headed like sundry sorts of wilde Beasts, but otherwise like Men and Women, their Apparel glistring, they come in making a riotous and unruly noise, with Torches in their hands.

COMUS
The Star that bids the Shepherd fold,
Now the top of Heav'n doth hold,
And the gilded Car of Day,
His glowing Axle doth allay
In the steep Atlantick stream,
And the slope Sun his upward beam

Shoots against the dusky Pole,
Pacing toward the other gole
Of his Chamber in the East.
Meanwhile welcom Joy, and Feast,
Midnight shout, and revelry,
Tipsie dance, and Jollity.
Braid your Locks with rosie Twine
Dropping odours, dropping Wine.
Rigor now is gon to bed,
And Advice with scrupulous head,
Strict Age, and sowre Severity,
With their grave Saws in slumber ly.
We that are of purer fire
Imitate the Starry Quire,
Who in their nightly watchfull Sphears,
Lead in swift round the Months and Years.
The Sounds, and Seas with all their finny drove
Now to the Moon in wavering Morrice move,
And on the Tawny Sands and Shelves,
Trip the pert Fairies and the dapper Elves;
By dimpled Brook, and Fountain brim,
The Wood-Nymphs deckt with Daisies trim,
Their merry wakes and pastimes keep:
What hath night to do with sleep?
Night hath better sweets to prove,
Venus now wakes, and wak'ns Love.
Com let us our rights begin,
'Tis onely day-light that makes Sin
Which these dun shades will ne're report.
Hail Goddesse of Nocturnal sport
Dark vaild Cotytto, t' whom the secret flame
Of mid-night Torches burns; mysterious Dame
That ne're art call'd, but when the Dragon woom
Of Stygian darknes spets her thickest gloom,
And makes one blot of all the ayr,
Stay thy cloudy Ebon chair,
Wherin thou rid'st with Hecat', and befriend
Us thy vow'd Priests, til utmost end
Of all thy dues be done, and none left out,
Ere the blabbing Eastern scout,
The nice Morn on th' Indian steep
From her cabin'd loop hole peep,
And to the tel-tale Sun discry
Our conceal'd Solemnity.
Com, knit hands, and beat the ground,
In a light fantastick round.

The Measure.

Break off; break off, I feel the different pace,
Of som chast footing neer about this ground.

Run to your shrouds, within these Brakes and Trees,
Our number may affright: Som Virgin sure
(For so I can distinguish by mine Art)
Benighted in these Woods. Now to my charms,
And to my wily trains, I shall e're long
Be well stock't with as fair a herd as graz'd
About my Mother Circe. Thus I hurl
My dazling Spells into the spungy ayr,
Of power to cheat the eye with blear illusion,
And give it false presentments, lest the place
And my quaint habits breed astonishment,
And put the Damsel to suspicious flight,
Which must not be, for that's against my course;
I under fair pretence of friendly ends,
And well plac't words of glozing courtesie
Baited with reasons not unplausible
Wind me into the easie-hearted man,
And hugg him into snares. When once her eye
Hath met the vertue of this Magick dust,
I shall appear som harmles Villager
Whom thrift keeps up about his Country gear,
But here she comes, I fairly step aside,
And hearken, if I may, her busines here.

The Lady enters.

LADY
This way the noise was, if mine ear be true,
My best guide now, me thought it was the sound
Of Riot, and ill manag'd Merriment,
Such as the jocond Flute, or gamesom Pipe
Stirs up among the loose unleter'd Hinds,
When for their teeming Flocks, and granges full
In wanton dance they praise the bounteous Pan,
And thank the gods amiss. I should be loath
To meet the rudenesse, and swill'd insolence
of such late Wassailers; yet O where els
Shall I inform my unacquainted feet
In the blind mazes of this tangl'd Wood?
My Brothers when they saw me wearied out
With this long way, resolving here to lodge
Under the spreading favour of these Pines,
Stept as they se'd to the next Thicket side
To bring me Berries, or such cooling fruit
As the kind hospitable Woods provide.
They left me then when the gray-hooded Eev'n
Like a sad Votarist in Palmers weed
Rose from the hindmost wheels of Phoebus wain.
But where they are, and why they came not back,
Is now the labour of my thoughts, 'tis likeliest
They had ingag'd their wandring steps too far,

And envious darknes, e're they could return,
Had stole them from me, els O theevish Night
Why shouldst thou, but for som fellonious end,
In thy dark lantern thus close up the Stars,
That nature hung in Heav'n, and fill'd their Lamps
With everlasting oil, to give due light
To the misled and lonely Travailer?
This is the place as well as I may guess,
Whence eev'n now the tumult of loud Mirth
Was rife and perfect in my list'ning ear,
Yet nought but single darknes do I find.
What might this be? A thousand fantasies
Begin to throng into my memory
Of calling shapes, and beckning shadows dire,
And airy tongues, that syllable mens names
On Sands and Shoars and desert Wildernesses.
These thoughts may startle well, but not astound
The vertuous mind that ever walks attended
By a strong siding champion Conscience.
O welcom pure-ey'd Faith, white-handed Hope,
Thou hovering Angel girt with golden wings.
And thou unblemish't form of Chastity,
I see ye visibly and now beleeve
That he, the Supreme good t'whom all things ill
Are but as slavish officers of vengeance,
Would send a glistring Guardian if need were
To keep my life and honour unassail'd.
Was I deceiv'd, or did a sable cloud
Turn forth her silver lining on the night?
I did not err, there does a sable cloud
Turn forth her silver lining on the night,
And casts a gleam over this tufted Grove.
I cannot hallow to my Brothers, but
Such noise as I can make to be heard farthest
Ile venter, for my new enliv'nd spirits
Prompt me; and they perhaps are not far off.

SONG.

Sweet Echo, sweetest Nymph that liv'st unseen
Within thy airy shell
By slow Meander's margent green,
And in the violet imbroider'd vale
Where the love-lorn Nightingale
Nightly to thee her sad Song mourneth well.
Canst thou not tell me of a gentle Pair
That likest thy Narcissus are?
O if thou have
Hid them in som flowry Cave,
Tell me but where
Sweet Queen of Parly, Daughter of the Sphear,

So maist thou be translated to the skies,
And give resounding grace to all Heav'ns Harmonies.

COMUS
Can any mortal mixture of Earths mould
Breath such Divine inchanting ravishment?
Sure somthing holy lodges in that brest,
And with these raptures moves the vocal air
To testifie his hidd'n residence;
How sweetly did they float upon the wings
Of silence, through the empty-vaulted night
At every fall smoothing the Raven doune
Of darknes till it smil'd: I have oft heard
My mother Circe with the Sirens three,
Amid'st the flowry-kirtl'd Naiades
Culling their Potent hearbs, and balefull drugs.
Who as they sung, would take the prison'd soul,
And lap it in Elysium, Scylla wept,
And chid her barking waves into attention.
And fell Charybdis murmur'd soft applause:
Yet they in pleasing slumber lull'd the sense,
And in sweet madnes rob'd it of it self,
But such a sacred, and home-felt delight,
Such sober certainty of waking bliss
I never heard till now. Ile speak to her
And she shall be my Queen. Hail forren wonder
Whom certain these rough shades did never breed
Unlesse the Goddes that in rurall shrine
Dwell'st here with Pan, or Silvan, by blest Song
Forbidding every bleak unkindly Fog
To touch the prosperous growth of this tall Wood.

LADY
Nay gentle Shepherd ill is lost that praise
That is addrest to unattending Ears,
Not any boast of skill, but extreme shift
How to regain my sever'd company
Compell'd me to awake the courteous Echo
To give me answer from her mossie Couch.

COMUS
What chance good Lady hath bereft you thus?

LADY
Dim darknes, and this heavy Labyrinth.

COMUS
Could that divide you from neer-ushering guides?

LADY
They left me weary on a grassie terf.

COMUS
By falshood. or discourtesie, or why?

LADY
To seek in vally som cool friendly Spring.

COMUS
And left your fair side all unguarded Lady?

LADY
They were but twain, and purpos'd quick return.

COMUS
Perhaps fore-stalling night prevented them.

LADY
How easie my misfortune is to hit!

COMUS
Imports their loss, beside the present need?

LADY
No less then if I should my brothers loose.

COMUS
Were they of manly prime, or youthful bloom?

LADY
As smooth as Hebe's their unrazor'd lips.

COMUS
Two such I saw, what time the labour'd Oxe
In his loose traces from the furrow came,
And the swink't hedger at his Supper sate;
I saw them under a green mantling vine
That crawls along the side of yon small hill,
Plucking ripe clusters from the tender shoots,
Their port was more then human, as they stood;
I took it for a faery vision
Of som gay creatures of the element
That in the colours of the Rainbow live
And play i'th plighted clouds. I was aw-strook,
And as I past, I worshipt: if those you seek
It were a journey like the path to Heav'n,
To help you find them.

LADY
Gentle villager
What readiest way would bring me to that place?

COMUS
Due west it rises from this shrubby point.

LADY
To find out that, good Shepherd, I suppose,
In such a scant allowance of Star-light,
Would overtask the best Land-Pilots art,
Without the sure guess of well-practiz'd feet,

COMUS
I know each lane, and every alley green
Dingle, or bushy dell of this wilde Wood,
And every bosky bourn from side to side
My daily walks and ancient neighbourhood,
And if your stray attendance be yet lodg'd,
Or shroud within these limits, I shall know
Ere morrow wake, or the low roosted lark
From her thatch't pallat rowse, if otherwise
I can conduct you Lady to a low
But loyal cottage, where you may be safe
Till further quest.

LADY
Shepherd I take thy word,
And trust thy honest offer'd courtesie,
Which oft is sooner found in lowly sheds
With smoaky rafters, then in tapstry Halls
And Courts of Princes, where it first was nam'd,
And yet is most pretended: In a place
Less warranted then this, or less secure
I cannot be, that I should fear to change it.
Eie me blest Providence, and square my triall
To my proportion'd strength. Shepherd lead on.--

The Two Brothers.

ELDER BROTHER
Unmuffle ye faint stars, and thou fair Moon
That wontst to love the travailers benizon,
Stoop thy pale visage through an amber cloud,
And disinherit Chaos, that raigns here
In double night of darknes, and of shades;
Or if your influence be quite damm'd up
With black usurping mists, som gentle taper
Though a rush Candle from the wicker hole
Of som clay habitation visit us
With thy long levell'd rule of streaming light.
And thou shalt be our star of Arcady,
Or Tyrian Cynosure.

YOUNGER BROTHER

Or if our eyes
Be barr'd that happines, might we but hear
The folded flocks pen'd in their watled cotes,
Or sound of pastoral reed with oaten stops,
Or whistle from the Lodge, or village cock
Count the night watches to his feathery Dames,
'Twould be som solace yet, som little chearing
In this close dungeon of innumerous bowes.
But O that haples virgin our lost sister
Where may she wander now, whether betake her
From the chill dew, amongst rude burrs and thistles?
Perhaps som cold bank is her boulster now
Or 'gainst the rugged bark of som broad Elm
Leans her unpillow'd head fraught with sad fears.
What if in wild amazement, and affright,
Or while we speak within the direfull grasp
Of Savage hunger, or of Savage heat?

ELDER BROTHER

Peace brother, be not over-exquisite
To cast the fashion of uncertain evils;
For grant they be so, while they rest unknown,
What need a man forestall his date of grief
And run to meet what he would most avoid?
Or if they be but false alarms of Fear,
How bitter is such self delusion?
I do not think my sister so to seek,
Or so unprincipl'd in vertues book,
And the sweet peace that goodnes boosoms ever,
As that the single want of light and noise
(Not being in danger, as I trust she is not)
Could stir the constant mood of her calm thoughts,
And put them into mis-becoming plight.
Vertue could see to do what vertue would
By her own radiant light, though Sun and Moon
Were in the salt sea sunk. And Wisdoms self
Oft seeks to sweet retired Solitude,
Where with her best nurse Contemplation
She plumes her feathers and lets grow her wings
That in the various bustle of resort
Were all too ruffled and sometimes impaired.
He that has light within his own deer brest
May sit i'th center, and enjoy bright day,
But he that hides a dark soul, and foul thoughts
Benighted walks under the mid-day Sun;
Himself is his own dungeon.

YOUNGER BROTHER

Tis most true
That musing meditation most affects

The pensive secrecy of desert cell,
Far from the cheerfull haunt of men, and herds,
And sits as safe as in a Senat house,
For who would rob a Hermit of his Weeds,
His few Books, or his Beads, or Maple Dish,
Or do his gray hairs any violence?
But beauty like the fair Hesperian Tree
Laden with blooming gold, had need the guard
Of dragon watch with uninchanted eye,
To save her blossoms, and defend her fruit
From the rash hand of bold Incontinence.
You may as well spred out the unsun'd heaps
Of Misers treasure by an out-laws den,
And tell me it is safe, as bid me hope
Danger will wink on Opportunity,
And let a single helpless maiden pass
Uninjur'd in this wilde surrounding wast.
Of night, or lonelines it recks me not,
I fear the dred events that dog them both,
Lest som ill greeting touch attempt the person
Of our unowned sister.

ELDER BROTHER
I do not, brother,
Inferr, as if I thought my sisters state
Secure without all doubt, or controversie:
Yet where an equall poise of hope and fear
Does arbitrate th'event, my nature is
That I encline to hope, rather then fear,
And gladly banish squint suspicion.
My sister is not so defenceless left
As you imagine, she has a hidden strength
Which you remember not.

YOUNGER BROTHER
What hidden strength,
Unless the strength of Heav'n, if you mean that?

ELDER BROTHER
I mean that too, but yet a hidden strength
Which if Heav'n gave it, may be term'd her own:
'Tis chastity, my brother, chastity:
She that has that, is clad in compleat steel,
And like a quiver'd Nymph with Arrows keen
May trace huge Forests, and unharbour'd Heaths,
Infamous Hills, and sandy perilous wildes,
Where through the sacred rayes of Chastity,
No savage fierce, Bandite, or mountaneer
Will dare to soyl her Virgin purity,
Yea there, where very desolation dwels
By grots, and caverns shag'd with horrid shades,

She may pass on with unblench't majesty,
Be it not don in pride, or in presumption.
Som say no evil thing that walks by night
In fog, or fire, by lake, or moorish fen,
Blew meager Hag, or stubborn unlaid ghost,
That breaks his magick chains at curfeu time,
No goblin, or swart faery of the mine,
Hath hurtfull power o're true virginity.
Do ye beleeve me yet, or shall I call
Antiquity from the old Schools of Greece
To testifie the arms of Chastity?
Hence had the huntress Dian her dred bow
Fair silver-shafted Queen for ever chaste,
Wherwith she tam'd the brinded lioness
And spotted mountain pard, but set at nought
The frivolous bolt of Cupid, gods and men
Fear'd her stern frown, and she was queen oth' Woods.
What was that snaky-headed Gorgon sheild
That wise Minerva wore, unconquer'd Virgin,
Wherwith she freez'd her foes to congeal'd stone?
But rigid looks of Chast austerity,
And noble grace that dash't brute violence
With sudden adoration, and blank aw.
So dear to Heav'n is Saintly chastity,
That when a soul is found sincerely so,
A thousand liveried Angels lacky her,
Driving far off each thing of sin and guilt,
And in cleer dream, and solemn vision
Tell her of things that no gross ear can hear,
Till oft convers with heav'nly habitants
Begin to cast a beam on th'outward shape,
The unpolluted temple of the mind.
And turns it by degrees to the souls essence,
Till all be made immortal: but when lust
By unchaste looks, loose gestures, and foul talk,
But most by leud and lavish act of sin,
Lets in defilement to the inward parts,
The soul grows clotted by contagion,
Imbodies, and imbrutes, till she quite loose
The divine property of her first being.
Such are those thick and gloomy shadows damp
Oft seen in Charnell vaults, and Sepulchers
Lingering, and sitting by a new made grave,
As loath to leave the body that it lov'd,
And link't it self by carnal sensualty
To a degenerate and degraded state.

YOUNGER BROTHER
How charming is divine Philosophy!
Not harsh, and crabbed as dull fools suppose,
But musical as is Apollo's lute,

And a perpetual feast of nectar'd sweets,
Where no crude surfet raigns.

ELDER BROTHER
List, list, I hear
Som far off hallow break the silent Air.

YOUNGER BROTHER
Me thought so too; what should it be?

ELDER BROTHER
For certain
Either som one like us night-founder'd here,
Or els som neighbour Wood-man, or at worst,
Som roaving robber calling to his fellows.

YOUNGER BROTHER
Heav'n keep my sister, agen agen and neer,
Best draw, and stand upon our guard.

ELDER BROTHER
Ile hallow,
If he be friendly he comes well, if not,
Defence is a good cause, and Heav'n be for us.

[Enter The attendant **SPIRIT** habited like a Shepherd.

That hallow I should know, what are you? speak;
Com not too neer, you fall on iron stakes else.

SPIRIT
What voice is that, my young Lord? speak agen.

YOUNGER BROTHER
O brother, 'tis my father Shepherd sure.

ELDER BROTHER
Thyrsis? Whose artful strains have oft delaid
The huddling brook to hear his madrigal,
And sweeten'd every muskrose of the dale,
How cam'st thou here good Swain? hath any ram
Slip't from the fold, or young Kid lost his dam,
Or straggling weather the pen't flock forsook?
How couldst thou find this dark sequester'd nook?

SPIRIT
O my lov'd masters heir, and his next joy,
I came not here on such a trivial toy
As a stray'd Ewe, or to pursue the stealth
Of pilfering Woolf, not all the fleecy wealth
That doth enrich these Downs, is worth a thought

To this my errand, and the care it brought.
But O my Virgin Lady, where is she?
How chance she is not in your company?

ELDER BROTHER
To tell thee sadly Shepherd, without blame
Or our neglect, we lost her as we came.

SPIRIT
Ay me unhappy then my fears are true.

ELDER BROTHER
What fears good Thyrsis? Prethee briefly shew.

SPIRIT
Ile tell ye, 'tis not vain or fabulous,
(Though so esteem'd by shallow ignorance)
What the sage Poets taught by th' heav'nly Muse,
Storied of old in high immortal vers
Of dire Chimera's and inchanted Iles,
And rifted Rocks whose entrance leads to hell,
For such there be, but unbelief is blind.
Within the navil of this hideous Wood,
Immur'd in cypress shades a Sorcerer dwels
Of Bacchus, and of Circe born, great Comus,
Deep skill'd in all his mothers witcheries,
And here to every thirsty wanderer,
By sly enticement gives his banefull cup,
With many murmurs mixt, whose pleasing poison
The visage quite transforms of him that drinks,
And the inglorious likenes of a beast
Fixes instead, unmoulding reasons mintage
Character'd in the Face; this have I learn't
Tending my flocks hard by i'th hilly crofts,
That brow this bottom glade, whence night by night
He and his monstrous rout are heard to howl
Like stabl'd wolves, or tigers at their prey,
Doing abhorred rites to Hecate
In their obscured haunts of inmost bowres.
Yet have they many baits, and guilefull spells
To inveigle and invite th' unwary sense
Of them that pass unweeting by the way.
This evening late by then the chewing flocks
Had ta'n their supper on the savoury Herb
Of Knot-grass dew-besprent, and were in fold,
I sate me down to watch upon a bank
With Ivy canopied, and interwove
With flaunting Hony-suckle, and began
Wrapt in a pleasing fit of melancholy
To meditate my rural minstrelsie,
Till fancy had her fill, but ere a close

The wonted roar was up amidst the Woods,
And fill'd the Air with barbarous dissonance,
At which I ceas' t, and listen'd them a while,
Till an unusuall stop of sudden silence
Gave respit to the drowsie frighted steeds
That draw the litter of close-curtain'd sleep.
At last a soft and solemn breathing sound
Rose like a steam of rich distill'd Perfumes,
And stole upon the Air, that even Silence
Was took e're she was ware, and wish't she might
Deny her nature, and be never more
Still to be so displac't. I was all eare,
And took in strains that might create a soul
Under the ribs of Death, but O ere long
Too well I did perceive it was the voice
Of my most honour'd Lady, your dear sister.
Amaz'd I stood, harrow'd with grief and fear,
And O poor hapless Nightingale thought I,
How sweet thou sing'st, how neer the deadly snare!
Then down the Lawns I ran with headlong hast
Through paths, and turnings oft'n trod by day,
Till guided by mine ear I found the place
Where that damn'd wisard hid in sly disguise
(For so by certain signes I knew) had met
Already, ere my best speed could praevent,
The aidless innocent Lady his wish't prey,
Who gently ask't if he had seen such two,
Supposing him som neighbour villager;
Longer I durst not stay, but soon I guess't
Ye were the two she mean't, with that I sprung
Into swift flight, till I had found you here,
But furder know I not.

YOUNGER BROTHER
O night and shades,
How are ye joyn'd with hell in triple knot
Against th'unarmed weakness of one Virgin
Alone, and helpless! Is this the confidence
You gave me Brother?

ELDER BROTHER
Yes, and keep it still,
Lean on it safely, not a period
Shall be unsaid for me: against the threats
Of malice or of sorcery, or that power
Which erring men call Chance, this I hold firm,
Vertue may be assail'd, but never hurt,
Surpriz'd by unjust force, but not enthrall'd,
Yea even that which mischief meant most harm,
Shall in the happy trial prove most glory.
But evil on it self shall back recoyl,

And mix no more with goodness, when at last
Gather'd like scum, and setl'd to it self
It shall be in eternal restless change
Self-fed, and self-consum'd, if this fail,
The pillar'd firmament is rott'nness,
And earths base built on stubble. But corn let's on.
Against th' opposing will and arm of Heav'n
May never this just sword be lifted up,
But for that damn'd magician, let him be girt
With all the greisly legions that troop
Under the sooty flag of Acheron,
Harpyies and Hydra's, or all the monstrous forms
'Twixt Africa and Inde, Ile find him out,
And force him to restore his purchase back,
Or drag him by the curls, to a foul death,
Curs'd as his life.

SPIRIT
Alas good ventrous youth,
I love thy courage yet, and bold Emprise,
But here thy sword can do thee little stead,
Farr other arms, and other weapons must
Be those that quell the might of hellish charms,
He with his bare wand can unthred thy joynts,
And crumble all thy sinews.

ELDER BROTHER
Why prethee Shepherd
How durst thou then thy self approach so neer
As to make this relation?

SPIRIT
Care and utmost shifts
How to secure the lady from surprisal,
Brought to my mind a certain Shepherd Lad
Of small regard to see to, yet well skill'd
In every vertuous plant and healing herb
That spreds her verdant leaf to th'morning ray,
He lov'd me well, and oft would beg me sing,
Which when I did, he on the tender grass
Would sit, and hearken even to extasie,
And in requitall ope his leather'n scrip,
And shew me simples of a thousand names
Telling their strange and vigorous faculties;
Amongst the rest a small unsightly root,
But of divine effect, he cull'd me out;
The leaf was darkish, and had prickles on it,
But in another Countrey, as he said,
Bore a bright golden flowre, but not in this soyl:
Unknown, and like esteem'd, and the dull swayn
Treads on it daily with his clouted shoon,

And yet more med'cinal is it then that Moly
That Hermes once to wise Ulysses gave;
He call'd it Haemony, and gave it me,
And bad me keep it as of sov'ran use
'Gainst all inchantments, mildew blast, or damp
Or gastly furies apparition;
I purs't it up, but little reck'ning made,
Till now that this extremity compell'd,
But now I find it true; for by this means
I knew the foul inchanter though disguis'd,
Enter'd the very lime-twigs of his spells,
And yet came Publick Officer if you have this about you
(As I will give you when we go) you may
Boldly assault the necromancers hall;
Where if he be, with dauntless hardihood,
And brandish't blade rush on him, break his glass,
And shed the lushious liquor on the ground,
But sease his wand, though he and his curst crew
Feirce signe of battail make, and menace high,
Or like the sons of Vulcan vomit smoak,
Yet will they soon retire, if he but shrink.

ELDER BROTHER
Thyrsis lead on apace, Ile follow thee,
And som good angel bear a sheild before us.

The scene changes to a stately Palace, set out with all manner of deliciousness; Soft Musick, Tables spred with all dainties. **COMUS** appears with his rabble. and the **LADY** set in an inchanted Chair, to whom he offers his Glass, which she puts by, and goes about to rise.

COMUS
Nay Lady sit; if I but wave this wand
Your nerves are all chain'd up in Alablaster,
And you a statue; or as Daphne was
Root-bound, that fled Apollo.

LADY
Fool do not boast,
Thou canst not touch the freedom of my minde
With all thy charms, although this corporal rinde
Thou haste immanacl'd, while Heav'n sees good.

COMUS
Why are you vext Lady? why do you frown
Here dwell no frowns, nor anger, from these gates
Sorrow flies farr: See here be all the pleasures
That fancy can beget on youthfull thoughts,
When the fresh blood grows lively, and returns
Brisk as the April buds in Primrose-season.
And first behold this cordial Julep here
That flames, and dances in his crystal bounds

With spirits of balm, and fragrant Syrops mixt.
Not that Nepenthes which the wife of Thone,
In Egypt gave to Jove-born Helena
Is of such power to stir up joy as this,
To life so friendly, or so cool to thirst.
Why should you be so cruel to your self,
And to those dainty limms which nature lent
For gentle usage, and soft delicacy?
But you invert the cov'nants of her trust,
And harshly deal like an ill borrower
With that which you receiv'd on other terms,
Scorning the unexempt condition
By which all mortal frailty must subsist,
Refreshment after toil, ease after pain,
That have been tir'd all day without repast,
And timely rest have wanted, but fair Virgin
This will restore all soon.

LADY
'Twill not false traitor,
'Twill not restore the truth and honesty
That thou hast banish't from thy tongue with lies
Was this the cottage, and the safe abode
Thou told'st me of? What grim aspects are these
These oughly-headed Monsters? Mercy guard me!
Hence with thy brew'd inchantments, foul deceit
Hast thou betrai'd my credulous innocence
With visor'd falshood, and base forgery,
And wouldst thou seek again to trap me here
With lickerish baits fit to ensnare a brute?
Were it a draft for Juno when she banquets,
I would not taste thy treasonous offer; none
But such as are good men can give good things,
And that which is not good, is not delicious
To a well-govern'd and wise appetite.

COMUS
O foolishnes of men! that lend their ears
To those budge doctors of the Stoick Furr,
And fetch their precepts from the Cynick Tub,
Praising the lean and sallow Abstinence.
Wherefore did Nature powre her bounties forth,
With such a full and unwithdrawing hand,
Covering the earth with odours, fruits, and flocks,
Thronging the Seas with spawn innumerable,
But all to please, and sate the curious taste?
And set to work millions of spinning Worms,
That in their green shops weave the smooth-hair'd silk
To deck her Sons, and that no corner might
Be vacant of her plenty, in her own loyns
She hutch't th'all-worshipt ore, and precious gems

To store her children with; if all the world
Should in a pet of temperance feed on Pulse,
Drink the clear stream, and nothing wear but Freize,
Th'all-giver would be unthank't, would be unprais'd,
Not half his riches known, and yet despis'd,
And we should serve him as a grudging master,
As a penurious niggard of his wealth,
And live like Natures bastards, not her sons,
Who would be quite surcharged with her own weight,
And strangl'd with her waste fertility;
Th'earth cumber'd, and the wing'd air dark't with plumes.
The herds would over-multitude their Lords,
The Sea o'refraught would swell, and th'unsought diamonds
Would so emblaze the forhead of the Deep,
And so bested with Stars, that they below
Would grow inur'd to light, and com at last
To gaze upon the Sun with shameless brows.
List Lady be not coy, and be not cosen'd
With that same vaunted name Virginity,
Beauty is natures coyn, must not be hoorded,
But must be currant, and the good thereof
Consists in mutual and partak'n bliss,
Unsavoury in th'injoyment of it self
If you let slip time, like a neglected rose
It withers on the stalk with languish't head.
Beauty is natures brag, and must be shown
In courts, at feasts, and high solemnities
Where most may wonder at the workmanship;
It is for homely features to keep home,
They had their name thence; course complexions
And cheeks of sorry grain will serve to ply
The sampler, and to teize the huswifes wooll.
What need a vermeil-tinctured lip for that
Love-darting eyes, or tresses like the Morn?
There was another meaning in these gifts,
Think what, and be adviz'd, you are but young yet.

LADY
I had not thought to have unlockt my lips
In this unhallow'd air, but that this Jugler
Would think to charm my judgement, as mine eyes,
Obtruding false rules pranckt in reasons garb.
I hate when vice can bolt her arguments,
And vertue has no tongue to check her pride:
Impostor do not charge most innocent nature,
As if she would her children should be riotous
With her abundance, she good cateress
Means her provision onely to the good
That live according to her sober laws,
And holy dictate of spare Temperance:
If every just man that now pines with want

Had but a moderate and heseeming share
Of that which lewdly-pamper'd Luxury
Now heaps upon som few with vast excess,
Natures full blessings would be well dispenc't
In unsuperfluous eeven proportion,
And she no whit encomber'd with her store,
And then the giver would he better thank't,
His praise due paid, for swinish gluttony
Ne're looks to Heav'n amidst his gorgeous feast,
But with besotted base ingratitude
Cramms, and blasphemes his feeder. Shall I go on?
Or have I said anough? To him that dares
Arm his profane tongue with contemptuous words
Against the Sun-clad power of Chastity,
Fain would I somthing say, yet to what end?
Thou hast nor Eare, nor Soul to apprehend
The sublime notion, and high mystery
That must be utter'd to unfold the sage
And serious doctrine of Virginity,
And thou art worthy that thou shouldst not know
More happiness then this thy present lot.
Enjoy your deer Wit, and gay Rhetorick
That hath so well been taught her dazling fence,
Thou art not fit to hear thy self convinc't;
Yet should I try, the uncontrouled worth
Of this pure cause would kindle my rap't spirits
To such a flame of sacred vehemence
That dumb things would be mov'd to sympathize,
And the brute Earth would lend her nerves, and shake,
Till all thy magick structures rear'd so high,
Were shatter'd into heaps o're thy false head.

COMUS
She fables not, I feel that I do fear
Her words set off by som superior power;
And though not mortal, yet a cold shuddring dew
Dips me all o're, as when the wrath of Jove
Speaks thunder, and the chains of Erebus
To som of Saturns crew. I must dissemble,
And try her yet more strongly. Com, no more,
This is meer moral babble, and direct
Against the canon laws of our foundation;
I must not suffer this, yet 'tis but the lees
And setlings of a melancholy blood;
But this will cure all streight, one sip of this
Will bathe the drooping spirits in delight
Beyond the bliss of dreams. Be wise, and taste.

The **BROTHERS** rush in with Swords drawn, wrest his Glass out of his hand, and break it against the ground; his rout make signe of resistance, but are all driven in; The attendant **SPIRIT** comes in.

SPIRIT

What, have you let the false enchanter scape?
O ye mistook, ye should have snatcht his wand
And bound him fast; without his rod revers't,
And backward mutters of dissevering power,
We cannot free the Lady that sits here
In stony fetters fixt, and motionless;
Yet stay, be not disturb'd, now I bethink me
Som other means I have which may he us'd
Which once of Meliboeus old I learnt
The soothest Shepherd that ere pip't on plains.
There is a gentle Nymph not farr from hence,
That with moist curb sways the smooth Severn stream,
Sabrina is her name, a Virgin pure,
Whilom she was the daughter of Locrine,
That had the Scepter from his father Brute.
The guiltless damsel flying the mad pursuit
Of her enraged stepdam Guendolen,
Commended her fair innocence to the flood
That stay'd her flight with his cross-flowing course,
The water Nymphs that in the bottom plaid,
Held up their pearled wrists and took her in,
Bearing her straight to aged Nereus Hall,
Who piteous of her woes, rear'd her lank head,
And gave her to his daughters to imbathe
In nectar'd lavers strew'd with Asphodil,
And through the porch and inlet of each sense
Dropt in Ambrosial Oils till she reviv'd,
And underwent a quick immortal change
Made Goddess of the River; still she retains
Her maid'n gentlenes, and oft at Eeve
Visits the herds along the twilight meadows,
Helping all urchin blasts, and ill luck signes
That the shrewd medling Elfe delights to make,
Which she with pretious viold liquors heals.
For which the Shepherds at their festivals
Carrol her goodnes lowd in rustick layes,
And throw sweet garland wreaths into her stream
Of pancies, pinks, and gaudy Daffadils.
And, as the old Swain said, she can unlock
The clasping charms, and thaw the numming spell,
If she be right invok't in warbled Song,
For maid'nhood she loves, and will be swift
To aid a Virgin, such as was her self
In hard besetting need, this will I try
And adde the power of som adjuring verse.

SONG.

Sabrina fair
Listen when thou art sitting

Under the glassie, cool, translucent wave,
In twisted braids of Lillies knitting
The loose train of thy amber-dropping hair,
Listen for dear honour's sake,
Goddess of the silver lake,
Listen and save.

Listen and appear to us
In name of great Oceanus,
By the earth-shaking Neptune's mace,
And Tethys grave majestick pace,
By hoary Nereus wrincled look,
And the Carpathian wisards hook,
By scaly Tritons winding shell,
And old sooth-saying Glaucus spell,
By Leucothea's lovely hands,
And her son that rules the strands,
By Thetis tinsel-slipper'd feet,
And the Songs of Sirens sweet,
By dead Parthenope's dear tomb,
And fair Ligea's golden comb,
Wherwith she sits on diamond rocks
Sleeking her soft alluring locks,
By all the Nymphs that nightly dance
Upon thy streams with wily glance,
Rise, rise, and heave thy rosie head
From thy coral-pav'n bed,
And bridle in thy headlong wave,
Till thou our summons answered have.
Listen and save.

SABRINA rises, attended by water-Nymphes, and sings.

SABRINA
By the rushy-fringed bank,
Where grows the Willow and the Osier dank,
My sliding Chariot stayes,
Thick set with Agat, and the azurn sheen
Of Turkis blew, and Emrauld green
That in the channell strayes,
Whilst from off the waters fleet
Thus I set my printless feet
O're the Cowslips Velvet head,
That bends not as I tread,
Gentle swain at thy request I am here.

SPIRIT
Goddess dear
We implore thy powerful hand
To undo the charmed band
Of true Virgin here distrest,

Through the force, and through the wile
Of unblest inchanter vile.

SABRINA
Shepherd 'tis my office best
To help insnared chastity;
Brightest Lady look on me,
Thus I sprinkle on thy brest
Drops that from my fountain pure,
I have kept of pretious cure,
Thrice upon thy fingers tip,
Thrice upon thy rubied lip,
Next this marble venom'd seat
Smear'd with gumms of glutenous heat
I touch with chaste palms moist and cold,
Now the spell hath lost his hold;
And I must haste ere morning hour
To wait in Amphitrite's bowr.

SABRINA descends, and the **LADY** rises out of her seat.

SPIRIT
Virgin, daughter of Locrine
Sprung of old Anchises line,
May thy brimmed waves for this
Their full tribute never miss
From a thousand petty rills,
That tumble down the snowy hills:
Summer drouth, or singed air
Never scorch thy tresses fair,
Nor wet Octobers torrent flood
Thy molten crystal fill with mudd,
May thy billows rowl ashoar
The beryl, and the golden ore,
May thy lofty head be crown'd
With many a tower and terrass round,
And here and there thy banks upon
With Groves of myrrhe, and cinnamon.

Com Lady while Heaven lends us grace,
Let us fly this cursed place,
Lest the Sorcerer us intice
With som other new device.
Not a waste, or needless sound
Till we com to holier ground,
I shall be your faithfull guide
Through this gloomy covert wide,
And not many furlongs thence
Is your Fathers residence,
Where this night are met in state
Many a friend to gratulate

His wish't presence, and beside
All the Swains that there abide,
With Jiggs, and rural dance resort,
We shall catch them at their sport,
And our sudden coming there
Will double all their mirth and chere;
Com let us haste, the Stars grow high,
But night sits monarch yet in the mid sky.

The Scene changes, presenting Ludlow Town and the President Castle, then com in Countrey-Dancers, after them the attendant **SPIRIT**, with the **TWO BROTHERS** and the **LADY**.

SONG.

SPIRIT
Back Shepherds, back, anough your play,
Till next Sun-shine holiday,
Here be without duck or nod
Other trippings to be trod
Of lighter toes, and such Court guise
As Mercury did first devise
With the mincing Dryades
On the Lawns, and on the Leas.

This second Song presents them to their **FATHER** and **MOTHER**.

Noble Lord, and Lady bright,
I have brought ye new delight,
Here behold so goodly grown
Three fair branches of your own,
Heav'n hath timely tri'd their youth.
Their faith, their patience, and their truth
And sent them here through hard assays
With a crown of deathless Praise,
To triumph in victorious dance
O're sensual folly, and Intemperance.

The dances ended, the **SPIRIT** Epiloguizes.

SPIRIT
To the Ocean now I fly,
And those happy climes that ly
Where day never shuts his eye,
Up in the broad fields of the sky:
There I suck the liquid ayr
All amidst the Gardens fair
Of Hesperus, and his daughters three
That sing about the golden tree:
Along the crisped shades and bowres
Revels the spruce and jocond Spring,
The Graces, and the rosie-boosom'd Howres,

Thither all their bounties bring,
That there eternal Summer dwels,
And West winds, with musky wing
About the cedar'n alleys fling
Nard, and Cassia's balmy smels.
Iris there with humid bow,
Waters the odorous banks that blow
Flowers of more mingled hew
Then her purfl'd scarf can shew,
And drenches with Elysian dew
(List mortals, if your ears be true)
Beds of Hyacinth, and roses
Where young Adonis oft reposes,
Waxing well of his deep wound
In slumber soft, and on the ground
Sadly sits th' Assyrian Queen;
But far above in spangled sheen
Celestial Cupid her fam'd son advanc't,
Holds his dear Psyche sweet intranc't
After her wandring labours long,
Till free consent the gods among
Make her his eternal Bride,
And from her fair unspotted side
Two blissful twins are to be born,
Youth and Joy; so Jove hath sworn.
But now my task is smoothly don,
I can fly, or I can run
Quickly to the green earths end,
Where the bow'd welkin slow doth bend,
And from thence can soar as soon
To the corners of the Moon.
Mortals that would follow me,
Love vertue, she alone is free,
She can teach ye how to clime
Higher then the Spheary chime;
Or if Vertue feeble were,
Heav'n it self would stoop to her.

www.ingramcontent.com/pod-product-compliance
Lightning Source LLC
Chambersburg PA
CBHW060145050426
42448CB00010B/2304